"Have you felt it—that deep longing for a genuine friendship? Me too! It's a natural part of being female. In her new book, Brenda Poinsett has masterfully uncovered the deep need of a woman's heart—to have a close friend. You know the kind; the one who will listen when our heart is full to bursting, who will let us cry on her shoulder even if we mess up her outfit, and who will give us that 'come to Jesus talk' when we need it. As a relationship coach, I know this book will be a great resource for my clients because life is all about authentic relationships."
—**Kathryn Robbins, relationship coach and president, Personality Principles, LLC**

D0369884

Endorsements

"Brenda Poinsett creatively captures what women have always known—women need women! Yet, she goes a step further offering guidance for each stage of life, ensuring we're engaged in healthy nurturing friendships for each step of the journey. You'll uncover renewed determination to make nurturing your friendships a key priority."
—Linda Lesniewski, women's minister, Green Acres Baptist Church

"Reading Brenda Poinsett's *The Friendship Factor* is like chatting with a dear friend. She explores the topic of friendship with energetic vigor, using examples from God's Word and her own intriguing life experiences. The reader is led to ponder her need for friendship and the benefits of true friendship, and the book climaxes with how-to lessons about friendship. Thanks, Brenda, for your enjoyable insights into one of life's sweetest blessings."
—Diana Davis, author, *Fresh Ideas for Women's Ministry*

"Brenda Poinsett captured my attention as she referred to this electronic age where one could have multiple Facebook friends, yet no one to connect and converse with on an intimate, face-to-face level. This book does not just scratch the surface, but rather delves into very practical, helpful insights concerning developing deep friendships with other girlfriends. Her 'circle the wagons' approach to women's ministry is very refreshing, using many personal, real-life illustrations. Brenda's strength of analysis and lens of experience make a winning combination, offering much-needed

encouragement as well as challenge to place the call to a girlfriend and issue the needed invitation, 'Let's do lunch.'"
—Pamela L. Buchanan, coordinator of women's ministries, Advent Christian General Conference

"Brenda Poinsett explores why husbands don't get it, but another ordinary woman, a 'verbal specialist,' can touch your feelings, join you in growing spiritually, and help you approach all the physical stages of life. Watch out! She may talk you into being a mentor to encourage other chicks."
—Edna Ellison, PhD, Christian mentoring guru, coauthor of *Woman to Woman: Preparing Yourself to Mentor* and 14 other small-group resources for women

"Finally! Brenda puts into writing the real reason women speak more words a day than men do—they need all those words to communicate with their girlfriends! We joke about women having to do everything en masse, but in reality God *designed* us to need each other. Not recognizing this natural outlet may stress not only our souls but also our family relationships. Brenda's careful research lends insight to biblical female relationships, allowing the reader to feel as though she were sharing a cup of java at Café Smadar with the likes of Hannah, Mary, Elizabeth, or Ruth—but she doesn't stop there. She reveals her research of postmodern women, their needs, and their desire for female support; and we are privy to what she discovers."
—Patti Thornton, director, General Baptist Women's Ministries

the
FRIENDSHIP
factor

*Why Women
Need Other Women*

by

Brenda Poinsett

NEW HOPE
PUBLISHERS
Birmingham, Alabama

New Hope® Publishers
P. O. Box 12065
Birmingham, AL 35202-2065
www.newhopepublishers.com
New Hope Publishers is a division of WMU®.

Library of Congress Cataloging-in-Publication Data

Poinsett, Brenda.
  The friendship factor : why women need other women / by Brenda
Poinsett.
    p. cm.
  ISBN-13: 978-1-59669-247-3 (sc)
  ISBN-10: 1-59669-247-2 (sc)
  1. Christian women--Religious life. 2. Female friendship--Reli-
gious aspects--Christianity. I. Title.

  BV4527.P635 2010
  241'.6762082--dc22

                                   2009045079

ISBN-10: 1-59669-247-2
ISBN-13: 978-1-59669-247-3
N094142 • 0310 • 3.5M1

Dedication

To

Jan Turner
and my friends and co-workers
at FBC St. Clair

Contents

Part 3 The *B's* of Friendship

Acknowledgments

There wouldn't be this book on connecting and conversation if it weren't for my friend, Jan Turner. When she invited me to speak one year at the pastors' wives' luncheon at the Missouri Baptist Convention, we brainstormed several possible subjects. She suggested *Coffee Cup Friendships*. Rather hesitantly, I said, "OK, I can talk about that." I had learned some important lessons about women and friendship when moving to Missouri so I was certain I could develop the content. I was hesitant, though, because I didn't think women had a need for insight and encouragement regarding connecting and conversing.

Jan circulated the subjects we decided on among several clergy wives, and they voted for *Coffee Cup Friendships*. Hmm, OK, some pastors' wives are interested in this subject, but that still didn't mean many women were. However, once I gave this speech, it led to many other invitations to talk about *Coffee Cup Friendships*. Eventually I saw that women needed help and encouragement in this area so a book on connecting and conversation was born.

Throughout the researching and writing, Jan provided a listening ear, prayer support, and resource supplier. She also read—and corrected!—the final draft as did my husband.

Bob, who was a great support, encourager and sounding board throughout the writing.

Besides, Jan and Bob, I also received support in some way (prayer, feedback, interest, etc.) from Barbara Popp, Mary Rose Fox, Barbara Williams, Janet Smith, Lorraine Powers, Vivian McCaughan, Annette Huber, Sue Johnson, Christina Kitson, Jim Poinsett, Joel Poinsett, and Ben Poinsett.

Cynthia Thomas, editorial coordinator of *Today's Christian Woman*, was helpful in locating a resource for me.

My sisters, Judy Mills and Linda Cochran, understood about my writing schedule with regards to our mother's care. I appreciate their flexibility and consideration in allowing me to get the book written. The WMU Council at First Baptist Church of St. Clair, Missouri, was also helpful in relieving me of some program details and assisting me in planning because of my need to write.

I also want to thank and acknowledge all the women who participated in my survey. I hope they—and you—will understand that I had to edit some of the comments to make them more readable. I trust I did not distort in any way what they were trying to say.

I want to thank New Hope Publishers for seeing this as a topic women need. I'm grateful to Joyce Dinkins, Ella Robinson, and Kathryne Solomon who made this book's message clearer and more readable.

I also thank the women who have enriched my life, some who are mentioned by name and the many who are not mentioned in the book. Writing this book was a trip in gratitude and humility as I've realized the importance women have played in my life, in being there at important times, in supporting me through various challenges, in contributing to who I am as a person, and in listening to me talk. I wish there were room to name them all, but that would have made the book way too long! I hope they will know, though, by this acknowledgment that I value them as I do all who helped me write this book.

1

Is It Just Me
or Do Women Need to Talk?

Our loud laughter must have been what prompted
others in the restaurant to stare. Over chicken
salad sandwiches, Debbie, Cathy, Holly, and I were
having a fast-paced, dynamic conversation. We were so in
sync that we often completed each others' sentences or said
the same thing at the same time. Naturally, each instance
called for a hi-five, and we laughed heartedly when our
hands met in the air.

I love high-spirited, fast-flowing conversations any time,
but this one had a special glow. It was the glow that accom-
panies a particular moment you know will never occur again.
I wanted to freeze the moment and hold on to it because I
was moving and Debbie, Cathy, and Holly were staying.

The moment's glow

It wasn't as if I would never see these three again. I was only
moving three hundred miles away, but the particular com-
position of this moment would never be repeated.

There was the spontaneity of the moment. Earlier that
morning I had said good-bye to Bob, my husband, as he
went on ahead to start a new job. Looking around at all

I had to pack, I thought, *I can't do this*, and I meant more than just putting things in boxes. I did what any self-respecting woman would do, I asked Debbie, Cathy, and Holly to meet me for lunch.

There was the history we shared that gave us an easy camaraderie. We lived in the same community and went to the same church. We had memories of teas, banquets, discussion groups, Sunday School classes, and Christmas caroling. We could mention a name and no one asked, "Who?"

Added to the spontaneity and history was a sense of earnestness because we knew our time together was limited. We wanted to make the most of this face-to-face conversation before I departed. Later in recalling the lunch, Debbie said, "It was similar to last get-togethers I've had with other friends when I've moved or they have moved. More is probably said in those final conversations than in thousands of others with the same people."

It was also who we were at the moment. I was married, the mother of three grown sons, an adjunct college instructor, a leader in our little church, a writer and a speaker. Cathy, Debbie, and Holly, also church leaders, were all single. Cathy and Debbie were both social workers, and Holly worked as a receptionist at the college where I taught.

These same components would never come together in exactly the same way again because we were all on the brink of change. I was moving and no longer would be teaching. Cathy and Debbie were starting graduate school. Cathy was aiming toward a master's degree in social work, and Debbie was going to seminary to get a master's in theology. Holly, a single mom, still living with her parents and needing both their emotional and financial support, was thinking about how she could become more independent and support her son on her own.

At some time or the other, we all face change. We may embrace it or resist it. We may lose our confident stride until we can get a handle on who we are going to be. Lisa, a friend in her late thirties, told me, "I always go kicking and screaming into the next stage of life." I know what she means. That's why I was resisting putting things into boxes. I didn't want to start over, and yet I was going to have to. As thoughts of what was ahead settled in on me, I knew I needed some girl talk. That's when I called Cathy, Debbie, and Holly, and asked, "Can you meet me for lunch?"

Power lunch

Interestingly, I said nothing about my reluctance to move or my fears associated with it once we got together, and yet I was strengthened by our talk and laughter. Our high-spirited conversation refreshed me emotionally and spiritually. I went home and started packing; it was time to get on with moving.

As you pack, you sort. Making choices about what to keep and what to discard is not a mechanical activity. Emotions and memories from your past parade before you. As I rummaged through years of living, I couldn't help but think about a woman's life, about how she grows and changes, about her needs, and about her relationships, particularly those with other women.

I found files from when Judy and I taught single young adults. Lots of memories were in between the manila folders—remnants of parties planned, retreats organized, and lessons taught.

I picked up a Bible given to me years ago by women in a prayer group. It was a time of discouragement for me—probably a time when I was facing change then too! They had sensed my discouragement, bought me a new Bible, and wrote their names inside. I looked at their names, recalled their faces, and remembered how I was loved and supported as we shared coffee, conversation, and prayer around the kitchen table.

I opened the china cabinet and found tucked in among the dishes favors from mother-daughter banquets and women's brunches. Among the treasures was a little golden spoon from Susan, who would be coming the next day to help me pack.

I smiled as I anticipated our time together. Even though she hadn't mentioned it, I knew she would bring lunch; that's just the way Susan is. As I wrapped the spoon in tissue paper, I thought of what our day together would be like. We would pack—and talk!—throughout the morning, then break for lunch and prayer. Talking and praying were two things we had been doing together for years. Our children were near each other in age. Through tears and laughter—and lunches!—we prayed them through junior high, high school, and into college. Our conversation would be more subdued than the conversation I had with Debbie, Cathy, and Holly—no high fives!—but just as valuable. I would be refreshed and strengthened by the conversation, for with Susan I would share my anxiety about the future.

The ringing of the telephone broke my reverie. It was Les, an older friend in her eighties. She was a friend who appreciated my matriarchal role and being included in family gatherings at our house. As we talked, we both admitted how much we were going to miss those gatherings. As I sat on the floor of my half-empty family room, we cried together—she on her end of the phone, and I on my end. As the tears flowed, I was reminded of how I needed women to cry as well as laugh and pray with me. It felt good to release the tears with someone who understood what I was feeling.

As I hung up, I sat where I was for a while. Having sorted through years of living, my mind was awhirl with thoughts about a woman's life, about the challenges and changes she faces, about her needs and her relationships, particularly those with other women. I realized how valuable it had been for me to connect with other women and to talk. I wondered, *Do other women need women in their life like this or is it just me? Do they need other women to help them deal with life's inevitable challenges? Do they need to share each other's tears, heartaches, pain and laughter?* I was intrigued, and I resolved right then and there to find out...just as soon as the move was over!

Call me curious

Before all the boxes were unpacked, I started asking women about what they needed from each other. Since I wasn't acquainted yet with local women, I wrote to females whom I had met in conferences and retreats. I asked them about where they were in life. *What challenges or changes are you facing? As you face these challenges, what kind of ministry do you need and want from other women? And when is experiencing this kind of ministry especially important to you?*

As I began receiving replies, I saw that having female friends to talk with was vital to a woman's sense of well being and for navigating change. And yet, some women admitted to not being able to make and to sustain those connections. I understood. There was a time when I thought finding and keeping friends just took care of itself. But a few years earlier, I had learned the hard way this is not always so, and perhaps that experience was contributing to my anxiety about moving. Would I find friends like Cathy, Debbie, Holly, Susan, and Les? How would I find them and how long would it take?

I function best when I understand the why of something, so I poured over the written answers I received. I read and reread the responses of 132 women ages 19 to 84. Eventually I also talked with women—first to Debbie and Cathy when they came to visit, and later, I led group discussions and interviewed women. I read books on adult development and relationships and studied the Bible to understand this phenomenon of women needing to connect and to converse.

It was an insightful, life-enriching experience that raised my appreciation for this part of a woman's nature, raised my consciousness about meeting this need in my own life, and helped me to understand how to work better with women.

- Where are you in your life?
- Are you in a transitional state?
- Do you need someone to talk with?
- Is there someone you can call for lunch?
- Is this something you have time for?
- Do you want to know yourself better?

Do you want to understand other women? The ones you work with? The ones you are involved with in church and community groups?

If you need support along the twists and turns of life, if you want to understand yourself better, or better understand other women, if you want to relate to them, minister to them and with them—and receive from them!—then join me for a look at what I learned about the power of conversation in women's lives.

Part 1

It's a Girl Thing

2

It Isn't Just Me!

Once very early on a stormy Sunday morning, I was having trouble sleeping. I was sick, and I kept tossing and turning, trying to find a comfortable niche. Noticing my movement was disturbing Bob's sleep, I left our bedroom and moved to the couch in the family room. As the wind blew and the rain fell outside, I heard all kinds of sounds. At one point, I thought I heard someone at the front door. *Surely, I'm imagining this; after all I have a fever.* Later I heard noises in the garage. Our "outside" cat spent his nights there so I wondered, *What has gotten into him?* Then the door from the garage to the kitchen opened. Now, in the darkness, I couldn't see the door open, but I could see the appearance of a very small light like a lighted cigarette. *Oh, my gosh, someone is in our house!* I pounded on the wall that separated our bedroom from the family room, and yelled, "Bob, Bob, someone's in our house!"

Bob came running and switched on a light. Sure enough, an intruder was in our house. When he saw Bob, he headed around the corner to our living room. Bob caught up with the guy, wrestled him to the floor and held him there. Bob yelled to our teenagers, who were awake by this time, "Get a rope." To me he shouted, "Call the police."

After a while the police came, recorded our statements, and took the intruder away. We made hot chocolate, sat, and pondered the experience together. Later, when Bob and the boys were leaving for church, Bob said, "Now don't say anything about this to anyone." I gulped. *You experience something like this, and you're not going to talk about it? You're going to go to church and not say a word to anyone?*

I was glad I was sick that morning and had to stay home! I couldn't have honored Bob's request. How about you? Would you have been able to keep quiet?

Have I got something to tell you!

When you receive news—good or bad—what do you want to do? When something unusual happens, what's your first impulse? For many women, our response is the same as Mary's when she found out she was pregnant. We find someone to tell.

After the angel Gabriel told young Mary she was going to be the mother of Jesus, *"soon afterward"* she headed toward her cousin Elizabeth's house (Luke 1:39a). She needed to talk about her unusual experience. She must have pinched herself on the way and asked herself: *Did I really see an angel? Did he really tell me that I am going to have God's child? Was I dreaming or was this real?*

When something unusual happens to us our impulse is to talk about it, to replay the experience. We can relive it and express our emotions about it. Talking can help us deal with the fallout and/or enrich our experience. The Bible suggests that it may have been enriching for Mary. It was *after* she arrived at Elizabeth's and shared her experience that she broke forth in song: *"My heart praises the Lord; my soul is glad...for he has remembered me, his lowly servant! From now on all people will call me happy"* (Luke 1:46–48).

While talking about the unusual is a natural response—and often an important one—some of us also need to talk about the *usual*, the ordinary things of life. You know what I mean if you've wanted to share your delight in something your child said or tell a neighbor about seeing goldfinches in your yard. You can understand if you have wanted to talk about an embarrassing moment you had in a restaurant, a new recipe you tried, a helpful magazine article you read, or your frustration with some new software.

I call this kind of talk "life processing," and my mother and I are good at it, especially after a large family gathering. We work together getting the meal ready for her children, their spouses, their children, grandchildren and great grandchildren, and sometimes cousins. We eat at noon and then have punch and cake in the afternoon or watermelon depending on the season. Around 3:30 people start leaving, making their way back home. By 5:00, it is just Mom, my father, Bob, and me left, and we warm the leftovers for a light supper. The men quickly eat and head to the living room to watch the evening news. That's when Mom says, "Want a cup of coffee?" I always answer, "Sure," because I know we are going to be sitting for a while.

As we sip coffee and nibble on some leftover pie, we talk about the day—the food, the children, the games, the laughter—whatever might have transpired. Some like my father would say, "It's a bunch of talk about nothing." Not to Mom and me, it isn't. Rather it's the capstone of the day, completing and rounding it out, giving us a satisfied feeling and enriching the experience.

I missed having someone to talk to about "a bunch of nothing" after I moved, not that I'm a big talker (something I think you ought to know as you read this book). As a teenager, I never stayed up talking into the wee hours of the night at slumber parties. I can soon get bored with conversations that don't seem to be going anywhere. I appreciate times of solitude, even crave it at times, but after I moved I had more solitude than I wanted. Thankfully, I had Bob to talk with when he was home, but his new job required day and night work. And even though he doesn't like to talk about intruders, my husband is a good conversationalist. He's not always interested, though, in the kinds of things I want and need to talk about. From time to time, I need girl talk, which became poignantly clear to me when I started shopping for carpet.

Connecting over carpet

Needing to replace some carpet, I started shopping at stores dealing in floor coverings. The place I returned to several times and finally bought the carpet from wasn't the store that had the best products. Rather I went back because of the female sales people. They gathered around me to help me select carpet. As they laid out samples on the floor for me to compare, I said, "I want something attractive but durable. I want something that can resists stains. You see my husband loves to eat cereal, but bless his heart, he always gets his bowl too full of milk. The milk sloshes over the edge of the bowl as he walks toward the television. I don't want to be a nagging wife. I don't want to say to him, 'You can't eat cereal on the new carpet!'"

When I said that, we clicked! The women started sharing their husband-children-food-carpet stories. For a little while on the floor, kneeling around the carpet samples, we became kindred spirits—just girls processing life together. I always felt better on the drive back home, ready to tackle boxes still waiting to be unpacked and ready to get on with adjusting to my new surroundings. It had the same effect as the power lunch with Cathy, Holly, and Debbie, even though I had no history with these women and wouldn't have further contact with them unless I bought more carpet!

This experience added to my reverie about the possible need women have to connect and to converse. This was something I had been pondering since packing to move. I kept wondering if it were just me or did other women have the same need so I wrote to women I had met at retreats and conferences. By now, their answers were coming in, and it was time to study them. What did the women say? Did any of them need to talk with other women as I did?

It's not just me!

Now my survey couldn't be classified as a scientific, and I can't even say it was balanced with input from all kinds of women from various backgrounds. Neither did the respondents have predetermined choices to select so I could tally their answers. After my carpet experience, I wished I had come right out and asked them, "Do you need to talk with other women?" Instead I had asked, "What ministry and nurturing do you need from other women?" The women could have written anything. As I flipped through their answers, I wondered if any of them mentioned directly or indirectly that they need to talk with other women.

I'll let you judge for yourself. Here are some of their answers.

"I need a friend, someone to hang out with, eat with, and just talk about life." Lisa, 19, single

"I need a friend who I can have fun with but who I can also talk with about what troubles me. I need someone I can vent with." Dana, 28, single

"I need a relationship that allows me to just call and say, 'I need to talk—NOW.'" Melissa, 28, married

"I need someone to talk to and share concerns with. I live far from family and have no close friends nearby. I would like a woman in my life to be a sounding board." Marla, 30, married with children

"I need someone with whom to talk about my feelings. Saying feelings out loud is therapeutic." Annie, 38, single

"I need to be able to express my concerns, heart-aches, faults, and failures to another woman." Kathy, 44, married with children

"I need encouragement. I need someone to go out for coffee with me and converse." Rhonda, 44, divorced with children

"I need women that will allow me to talk and who will listen." Terry, 45, married with children

"I need someone I can talk to about the Lord and go to women's things with me." Patty, 46, married with children

"At times, I need a listening ear even when I seem senseless." Donna, 60, married with children

"I need friends to visit with even though my church family is very supportive." Doris, 67, widowed with children

"What I need is someone to call and tell about my troubles and uncertainties." Mary, 77, widowed with children

So what do you think? Are there enough answers here for you to conclude that women need to talk to each other? There were more that alluded to this need, some of which I will share with you later in the book, but for now are you convinced? I was. Their comments were enough for me to conclude, *It isn't just me!*

I should have realized this sooner from the research that I did for *I'm Glad I'm a Woman* (Tyndale House Publishers), a book I wrote about the uniqueness of women. Talking is certainly not unique to women, but it does seem to be our specialty.

Verbal specialists

Conversation may be a vital part of women's lives because God designed us to be verbal specialists. He made us proficient with words. The human brain is divided front to back into two roughly symmetrical halves called the cerebral hemispheres. The right and left hemispheres have different specialties. Organizing space is one of the specialties of the right hemisphere. We use it when we solve jigsaw puzzles, design houses, plan gardens, recognize faces, paint pictures, and process our emotions. The left hemisphere is our speech center. It controls language and reading skills.

In some studies, men have been shown to be primarily right-hemisphere oriented, and women left-hemisphere oriented. While both sexes use both hemispheres, each sex "leans" more on one hemisphere than the other.

Females are primarily left-hemisphere oriented, and since the left hemisphere is our speech center, you can guess what our specialty is! Females have an advantage in almost all verbal skills: verbal reasoning, grammar, written prose, reading, languages, and talking! If you have been or are the mother of boys and girls, then you are aware of this difference. This verbal specialty shows up at a very young age. Female infants speak sooner, have larger vocabularies, and rarely demonstrate speech defects. Stuttering, for instance, occurs almost exclusively among boys. Girls read sooner,

> Females are primarily left-hemisphere oriented, and since the left hemisphere is our speech center, you can guess what our specialty is!

learn foreign languages more easily, and are more likely to enter occupations involving language mastery.

Because our verbal proficiency shows up at an early age, perhaps that's why many of us have learned to deal with life—and even enhance our life—by talking.

In lonely times and in not so lonely times, in bad times and good times, when we are young and when we are old, when we are single and when we are married, we women need to talk to each other. Shelley E. Taylor, in her book, *The Tending Instinct* (New York: Times Books, Henry Holt and Company, 2002), says, "The primary activity that women enjoy together is talking." It's not just me; *it's us*! Now that is something I want to tell, which is why I am writing this book.

What women need

When my consciousness was raised about women needing to talk, I was motivated to connect with others and make time for conversations instead of waiting and hoping it would happen. I want to encourage others to do the same.

You don't have to have "just moved" to be lonely. Many people these days are lonely. Holly Vicente Robaina, in the article "Isolation Nation," (*Today's Christian Woman*, July/August 2007) repeats statistics from the Social Isolation in America study published in the June 2006 issue of *American Sociological Review* that one out of every four persons doesn't have a single friend to turn to in times of need. In a 2007 poll by *Today's Christian Woman* magazine, 42 percent of the women said they were lonely often or constantly.

You don't have to have just moved to be lonely. You can have people around you, living a busy, active life, and yet in the midst of it all, still feel like something is missing. It may be that you want the relaxation, the refreshment, the power, or the life enrichment that comes with connecting and talking with other women. This is not a weakness on your part or a frivolous desire; you have a legitimate need, and one I'm encouraging you to respond to.

Whether you are lonely or busy or both, I trust that raising your consciousness about this need will do for you what it did for me. It spurred me to action, and I think it will do the same for you.

3

Can You Meet Me for Lunch?

Oh, the joy of talking! Women take a lot of teasing about our verbal specialty, but it is a wonderful proficiency to have. I first realized this when a young man in a Sunday School class Bob and I taught had an extremely hard time expressing himself. Because of some physical or psychological impairment, John spoke very slowly. His struggle to talk was obvious in the contortions of his cheeks, the twisting of his lips, and the wrinkling of his brow. His whole face was involved in trying to speak. Many people didn't have the patience to wait for John's words. Because of his slowness to speak, John was accused of being shy, incompetent, and stupid. John told me he had been cussed out in a checkout lane at a discount store because he couldn't get his words out fast enough.

After I taught a lesson on prayer, John stopped by our home in the middle of the day, in the middle of the week. I was puzzled by this, as he usually only visited when everyone was home. I invited him in, and John started talking. As usual, his words were slow and disconnected, almost as if he were handing me pieces of a jigsaw puzzle. As I sat listening, trying to put the pieces together, I tried to figure out what he wanted. There had to be a reason for his visit.

Then I remembered the lesson I had taught. *Could this have something to do with prayer?* So when he finished, I said, "Would you like me to pray for you?"

John nodded his head yes. I took the puzzle pieces, put them together as best as I could, and gave his problem to the Lord. When I finished, I looked at John. Tears were rolling down his cheeks. He thanked me and hugged me and then hugged me again. I felt like I was the one who should have been thanking him. John's gratitude made me realize what a blessing it is to be a verbal specialist.

With our verbal ability, women can pray fluently! We can verbalize our needs, praises, and intercessions to God! We can share the good news of the gospel. We can tell others what is wrong or what is right! We can formulate sentences and deliver them with ease; we can describe our experiences. We don't have to rely on expletives; we are able to say how we feel. We are able to articulate our problems and brainstorm solutions. How blessed women are to be so verbal, but this blessing doesn't come without challenges.

Oh, the challenges!

One temptation we have is to overuse this gift by talking too much. For some women, their left hemispheres seem to work overtime! The heightened activity of their left brain's specialty seems to diminish their sensitivity to the reception of their words. They dominate conversations, and they don't seem to realize when they are boring people or notice them turning away.

Another challenge we have is to use this verbal strength in the right way. The Bible has much to say about the power of words and the appropriate use of them. This gift God has blessed us with can be used for good and for evil. With our verbal specialty, we have the power to encourage and enrich the lives of others, but we also have the power to destroy with words (James 3:2–13).

Another challenge is finding a listener. Every talker needs a listener. We want someone to hear us when we speak. If talking is to be the joy that I believe God meant it to be, we need people to hear us. If you have ever had something you really wanted to express, and there was no one around to listen or at least no one you thought would be receptive, you know what I mean. The words get stuck in your throat, and lodge themselves there like a grape peeling, making you uncomfortable and distressed. I think Holly was speaking for many women when she wrote in her survey: *"the kind of ministry I need from another woman is just someone to talk with and to listen…Sometimes an ear is all I need."*

While all talkers, male and female, appreciate having listeners, there's an extra wrinkle involved for us. Most women not only want to be heard as in volume and clarity, but they want to be listened to. We want to sense that others are caring, supporting, or identifying with us as we talk. Women want to tap an "I-know-how-you-feel" response from their listeners.

Being listened to

We can tell if we are being listened to by what is said and by what is not said. The appropriate words voiced back in response to what we say are important in determining if we are being understood. Our listener's questions and comments help us access whether we are getting our meaning across or leaving out any important details. We can't say enough about the importance of words in conversations, but being listened to involves more than words. It also involves nonverbal clues.

We judge our listener's response by her laughter or by the sympathetic noises she makes. Or the evidence could be on our listener's face and in her eyes. Her eyes may crinkle up at the corners. Tears may trickle down her cheeks.

As you put together the verbal and nonverbal clues—and you may or may not be conscious of the process—you determine if you are being listened to. A sense of being heard will rise up within you. A bonding will take place, and you will know your listener is with you in spirit. Something washes over you so you feel relieved, refreshed, and at times, even spiritually renewed.

Since being listened to involves more than words, it is more apt to take place when you can see the other person. In face-to-face encounters, we can gauge what kind of attention our words are receiving. We can see if the listener is looking at us or elsewhere. We can judge if she is attentive. Is she being distracted? Is she quick to interrupt? Or does she change the subject? We can see her facial expressions and are close enough to hear if there is any intake of the breath or even a slight gasp. Assessing these things help us feel listened to more than other ways of communicating.

Emailing, phoning, and text messaging are fine for quick communication. They are so helpful for transmitting information, for keeping up with each other's schedules, and staying in contact. But sometimes in phone conversations you don't have the complete attention of the person on the other end., In "Technology Has Us So Plugged Into Data, We Have Turned Off" (*The Wall Street Journal*, November 10, 2003), Dennis K. Berman says, "The brainy people who study these things call this phenomenon 'absent presence.'" In other words, the person on the other end is there but she's not really with you. During a phone conversation, she may be saying *OK*, *right*, and *sure* while checking her email or researching something on the Internet. In these days, when women take pride in multitasking, you never know what is happening on the other end of the connection. You might hear cabinet doors shutting and closing or water running. I swear once I heard a commode flush in the background!

When we have a history with a person, we may assume we are being listened to when we send off an email message of distress, but it may be our assumption that is ministering to us instead. The person who received your email may or may not identify with you. Because of the bombardment of "needy" emails that she receives, she may quickly type back a sympathetic message such as "my prayers are with you" without any emotional involvement on her part whatsoever. You can't see her, so you don't know for sure.

Time also seems to be a factor in being listened to—time to draw out, amplify, and enhance what we are saying. You can't just say something and immediately receive back an "I-know-how-you-feel" response.

Once when I was being interviewed on the radio show *Moody Mid-day Connection*, one of the callers had a very complicated problem. I could not "hear" her although volume wasn't the problem. I couldn't get to the point when I could say, "I understand. I know how you feel."

> Hope is born within us when someone really listens… the world looks better and the challenges we face are not so formidable.

I tried to draw her out with questions, but as we talked, her problem got more and more complicated. And it was a highly pressured conversation since thousands of people were listening. As time was running out, I said, "This is too complicated to solve over the air. I wish I could have you in my home. Over coffee at my kitchen table, we could examine your situation strand by strand."

Slowing down with a hot cup of coffee, in an unhurried, face-to-face setting, we would have time to unwrap her need, and I could give her the gift of being listened to. Would I have been able to offer her a solution? Maybe. Maybe not. But I could give her hope, which is one of the significant outcomes of being listened to.

Hope is born within us when someone really listens. When we've been listened to, the world looks better and the challenges we face are not so formidable. When we press our hands against a steaming cup of coffee, slow down and talk things out, our attitude changes. In this way, having coffee together becomes a ministry.

Table ministry

When the home of Marge's neighbor caught fire, the kitchen had to be completely gutted. After some extensive remodeling, Marge took her little sons to visit the neighbor and to see the new kitchen. A table had not yet been bought but the new cabinets and appliances were all in place. Marge's five-year-old son looked all around, intently studying the room. Marge was puzzled by a child taking such interest. She wondered what he was thinking. Finally he said to the neighbor, "How can you see each other's eyes?"

Now it was the neighbor's turn to be puzzled, but his question cleared things up for Marge. At her house, Marge had been teaching her sons to converse while they were eating at the kitchen table. Time and time again, she said, "Now look at me while you are talking." No wonder this little fellow was wondering how the neighbors were ever going to converse if they didn't have a table. I tend to agree.

Seeing the eyes of the talker/listener works best for me when there's a table between us. A table has been my "altar of choice" as I've ministered to women through the years. The geographic location and circumstances changed from time to time but usually there was a table to accommodate conversation. We could see each other's eyes as we processed life and faith over coffee or lunch.

When my two older sons were infants and toddlers, the menu was toast, butter, jelly and coffee. The toast was for the kids, and the coffee was for my neighbor Carolyn and me as we all frequently sat around the table together. After I moved away, Carolyn, wrote, "I haven't met the new neighbors yet. I know if I were to go into their house and see the kitchen table, I would start crying as I would remember jelly smears and our many conversations."

When Ben, our third child, was a preschooler, it was coffee every weekday morning with my neighbor, Bettie. Ben and Bettie's son, Bruce, played while we had coffee and talked. We were both hard working women and by 10:00 we were ready for a 30-minute break. Over coffee, we talked and solved problems such as how to raise strong-willed boys! At times, I'll admit I wondered, *Can you raise children without coffee talk?*

When our sons were older in junior high and high school, I graduated to a leisurely lunch about every three weeks with Susan, whom I mentioned in chapter 1. Now that my sons are grown, I keep a more rigid work schedule, and having lunch in a restaurant with someone works well. The noon hour, when you would normally take a work break, becomes a small window of opportunity for conversation and connecting. This is a short window compared to the one that Mary and Elizabeth had together. They had a three-month-long window (Luke 1:56) but a lunch hour works well for many of today's time-pressed women. It gives them an opportunity for conversing where they can see each other's eyes. It works so well that when a woman calls and says, *Can you meet me for lunch?* you know what she wants. She wants to connect; she wants to talk.

When you need to talk

Meeting for lunch to connect and to converse is such an understood concept among women that I am going to use it as a metaphor in this book. It is going to stand for women taking time-out for unhurried, face-to-face conversation. This is not to say that food is completely irrelevant! Food can add nourishment and warmth to the occasion, but having lunch is a symbol of the slowing down process that facilitates our time-out. I mean, who can eat salad or soup fast?

Sipping coffee or tea together does the same thing because you slow down. You can't drink coffee fast—it was meant to be imbibed slowly. Over coffee or while sipping tea, for a little while, time stands still giving women time to talk and time to listen.

The same effect could be achieved by licking ice cream cones, taking a walk, or sipping lemonade in a porch swing together. Conversation can occur while doing crafts together as I imagine it occurred while Dorcas and her group of widows sewed for the poor (Acts 9:36–42). I can only imagine the many things they discussed as they met together. They may have stitched their lives back together after their losses as they stitched clothing for the poor. No wonder the other women were distraught at her death. They not only loved her, they had lost their lifeline.

Retreats, conferences, and girls' weekends offer the same possibilities: you get away from your regular life, slow down your pace, talk and listen to each other. Women from one church went to a Women of Faith conference and decided what they liked best was getting to be with the women of their own church. The next year instead of going to the Women of Faith conference, they rented rooms at a hotel and talked the night away! I'm not recommending this approach, but what I am suggesting is that many women want and need face-to-face conversations. As Laura, one of the survey respondents so wistfully put it, "I wish I had a woman in my life who would take time, really listen, not pressure me and give me some unhurried nurturing."

Whether it is crafts, exercise, beverages, or lunch, we can meet and nurture each other by slowing down, talking, looking each other in the eye and listening to each other. In the getting together, burdens are lifted. Confidences are shared. Secrets are told. Triumphs are celebrated. Problems are solved. And when the lunch hour is over, when the window of opportunity closes, a woman who has been listened to will feel she has been ministered to. These are times when we can experience the joy of talking and the satisfaction of being listened to.

4

A Girl's Gotta Share

Recently when my mom was staying with me, we received word that one of her nephews had been diagnosed with kidney and bone cancer. Naturally we were distressed and grieved over this. We were concerned for both Rick and his mother (my mother's sister) who lived with Rick. When several days went by with no further information about how Rick was getting along, we called a cousin whose farm was close to Rick's.

"Hi, Gerald. I have my mom here on the phone, and we both are wondering about Rick. How's he doing?"

"Have you heard the latest?" asked Gerald.

"What do you mean the latest? We heard he had kidney and bone cancer. Is there something besides that?"

"His barn burned down Saturday night."

"You're kidding!"

"No, his barn burned completely to the ground. It was a total loss. Inside he had two tractors, a truck, a combine, and a wagon full of grain. Everything was destroyed."

As we hung up, my mind was filled with the news of this loss and what it would mean in the life of this farmer and his elderly mother. The cancer diagnosis was awful enough, and now the instruments of his livelihood were destroyed.

Mom was clearly agitated by the news. She looked at me and said, "What friend can I call?"

"What?"

"Who can I call? I've got to tell someone about Rick."

Since her retirement, Mom had shared the ups and downs of life with friends who regularly dropped by her house and by lengthy phone conversations. And so on this occasion, she felt compelled to handle the distressing news the way she had always done—by sharing it with a friend. She insisted we call someone back where she lived. There are just times when a girl's gotta share.

Have I got news!

You know the feeling I'm writing about. It is an urgency, an inner compulsion, that makes you want to talk with someone who will understand and appreciate what you are saying.

This feeling may have occurred when you learned you were pregnant. You were elated that you were going to have a baby. Or maybe it occurred when you found out you weren't pregnant. You were relieved because you didn't know if your household could stretch to include another child.

It could be finally landing an important contract for your company. It was one that you had been working on for months, and the signing called for a relaxing moment at a tea room with a friend. Together you celebrated and savored the victory.

It could be finding something you lost like the woman in Jesus' story who found the lost coin (Luke 15:8–10). She had to share her good news. She called her friends and neighbors together, and said to them, "*I am so happy I found the coin I lost. Let us celebrate!*" (Luke 15:9).

It could be distressing news when you need to sort out

your emotions or shocking news that leaves you reeling, when you wonder if life will ever be normal again.

It could be when you have had a spirited disagreement with your husband, a child or a friend, and you are blown away by it. You need someone to tell so you can vent your emotions without escalating the disagreement.

Why is it that at times like these, we often use the word *share* as in "I need to share something with you"? Wouldn't the word *talk* work just as well? Possibly, but I think we use *share* because we have more than words in mind. We're also thinking about emotions such as the joy of pregnancy, the sadness of loss or the anger stewing from a disagreement. We may also want someone to enter into what we are experiencing—to share the moment with us. We may want to give not only the facts but our interpretation of the facts! As we share, we give up something. When the conversation is over, the listener will have a part of us, some of our emotions or a portion of the experience.

We can best judge if this happens in face-to-face conversations where we can detect if we are getting the "I-know-how-you-feel" response. If we do, we know that sharing has occurred. The listener "gets it." She understands where we are coming from or why we are feeling the way we do. She may or may not say, "I know how you feel." Instead, she may say: "I know what you mean"; "I understand"; or "I would feel the same way if I were you." Or she may not say anything, but something about her expression will let you know she "gets it."

When sharing occurs, the teller has a sense that her listener understands, grasps, and appreciates what she is experiencing. The teller knows she has been "listened to," and when the conversation is over, she no longer owns it all. She has given away part of herself, which may sound like she loses, but she doesn't. Even though we give up something, we gain something in return when we share.

Dividing to add

What we gain varies from person to person and according to what is shared.

We may gain relief from expressing what is bothering us or perplexing us. It just feels so good to talk about it, and it is a relief not to have to keep it bottled up inside.

When we share a burden, we gain a lighter load. The burden is no longer as heavy. This doesn't mean the burden goes away, but it means it weighs less; therefore, it easier to carry.

When we share a problem, we gain a better look at it. There's just something about getting it outside of ourselves that improves our vision. Plus we gain the support of the person we're talking with, and then we feel better equipped to deal with the problem.

When we share our failures, we may gain the confidence to keep trying. Pamela wrote, "I need someone that I can honestly share my failures with....I don't want to have to give the impression that everything is OK when it's not." Pamela is in the "earnest years" of life, something we'll talk more about in chapter 10. This is the time of life when we strive hard to succeed, a time when we can get caught up in trying to please bosses, co-workers, family members, and fellow Christians. Sometimes in the trying, we fail. Oh, the self-reproach that can be involved, but if we can honestly share with another person, we can be affirmed and encouraged. "It's OK, girl, you meant well. Your intentions were the best."

Something else we may gain from sharing is forgiveness. We never get to a place when we are beyond temptation, and if we succumb, we may feel terrible about it. When we share our guilt with a Christian friend, she can be God's agent to administer the soothing balm of forgiveness (John 20:22–23). She may not even say the word *forgive*, but it will be evident in her eyes, her mannerisms, and her listening. As she gives back that "I-know-how-you-feel" response, you know that you are not the only one who sins, and you are forgiven.

One of the things I often hope to gain from sharing—and I may be the odd person out on this—is having someone to commiserate with me. I know, I know, that sounds like I want someone to share my misery, doesn't it? I don't want her to be miserable, but I want someone to ponder life with me. I want someone who is not in a hurry to listen intently, look me in the eye, and perhaps utter something like:

- *You've got to be kidding!*
- *I can't believe what you are telling me,* or
- *I never thought this would happen to you.*

Or maybe she could just sit in silence with me as we sip coffee together. I see this as what Job's friends did for him *initially*. They came and sat with him after he had experienced catastrophic losses (Job 2:11–13). They wanted to *"sympathize with him and comfort him"* (Job 2:11 NIV). *"They sat on the ground with him for seven days and seven nights. No one said a word to him, because they saw how great his suffering was"* (Job 2:13 NIV). Now that is remarkable! It is rare to find someone who can or who is willing to sit with you and contemplate life. And when you do, you gain a soothing balm for your soul.

Sharing also provides a way to gain control of troubling emotions. Emotions such as anger, grief, and jealousy are very powerful, and when we express those to others, the emotions lose some of their power. They are no longer as intense or damaging. But if we are not careful, and if our listener identifies too strongly with these emotions, they can escalate. Sharing multiplies as well as adds.

When dividing multiplies

My personal experience has been that when I share negative emotions, they lessen in their intensity, but there's always the case of the children of Israel to remind us that negative emotions multiply.

The foreigners traveling with the Israelites started grumbling. They were tired of the daily supply of bland manna. They wanted some chewy meat, crunchy vegetables, and flavorfully spiced foods. As they recalled the tasty meat and fish they had had in Egypt where they could have all they wanted, they activated the memories of the Israelites. Then the Israelites too began to complain. *"In Egypt we used to eat all the fish we wanted, and it cost us nothing. Remember the cucumbers, the watermelons, the leeks, the onions, and the garlic we had? But now our strength is gone. There is nothing at all to eat—nothing but this manna day after day!"* (Numbers 11:5–6). The complaints of the foreigners and the Israelites escalated as they shared their memories. They griped and complained as they stood around their tent entrances, causing Moses, their leader, great distress.

Multiplying negative emotions through sharing can occur, but more importantly, the positive ones can multiply Sharing takes away the loneliness of life and helps us grasp its joys and pleasure. Sharing with a friend or friends your joy or happiness enhances your life, magnifies your feelings, and gives you opportunities to celebrate.

When the angel Gabriel told Mary that she was going to have a miracle child, Mary felt compelled to go see Elizabeth, yet she lived somewhere in Judea. Mary lived in Nazareth of Galilee and to get to Elizabeth, she would have had to travel a distance of perhaps as much as 80 miles and go through Samaria. This would have been quite a daunting trip for a young woman in the beginning of a pregnancy to travel alone.

Mary could have sent a letter, about the only other means she had to communicate with Elizabeth, but that would have taken time. There was no postal system in operation for the average citizen, so she couldn't drop a letter in a mailbox down the street. The Romans had a postal system for government communication but not for general citizenry. A person had to find someone who was going that way to take a letter to someone. Phoebe, for example, carried Paul's letter to the church at Rome (Romans 16:1–2). Sending a letter might take weeks, and Mary's news couldn't wait. Remember that urgency to tell that I mentioned earlier!

Besides, if Mary sent her news via a letter, she would miss the joy of sharing. Mary didn't want to miss the look on Elizabeth's face when she told her about the angel and about her pregnancy. She would have missed seeing Elizabeth's face break into a smile as she pulled her in the door and hugged her. She would have been prevented from reliving the experience over and over in the days ahead with Elizabeth hanging on to every word. She would have missed the wonder of sharing.

> Mary didn't want to miss the look on Elizabeth's face when she told her about the angel and about her pregnancy.

Years ago Cicero wrote about the wonder of sharing. He said it affects both joys and sorrows. Joys are increased by being shared, while sorrows are decreased. Perhaps this is why the apostle Paul encouraged us to *"Be happy with those who are happy, weep with those who weep"* (Romans 12:15).

Once you've experienced the benefits of sharing, you will find yourself wanting to repeat the experience again when troubling times or good times occur. This is something you may not even have realized; you may only know that at certain times you have an impulse to call a friend and say, "Can you meet me for lunch? Have I got something to tell you!" We don't make this call to just anybody because we don't regard all conversations as sharing. Talking doesn't always equal sharing.

When talking is not sharing

You may have a wide circle of acquaintances, some closer to you than others, but if you are like me, you don't share with them all.

Some of your acquaintances may not be good listeners. They interrupt; they jump in with what is happening or has happened to them, never letting you finish your sentences. They don't look at you when you are talking. You can clearly tell their mind is somewhere else so it is obvious you will not receive an "I-know-how-you-feel" response.

Some people are dumpers; they unload on you. Sharing doesn't mean unloading. The person who dumps wants all the advantages of sharing from *you*, but once they have taken advantage of your good listening and taken up your time, then they are on their way. As they exit, they might even say, "You can pray about this," and assume you will without ever slowing down long enough to see what your reaction is.

And some of your acquaintances may be so into themselves that they may not identify with you, something necessary for sharing to occur. Jolene (not her real name) is one of those women. When our paths first crossed after I moved, I thought I would like her to be more than an acquaintance because of the interesting life she lives. I admired her and I often told her so.

After several conversations with her, I changed my mind about wanting her to be more than an acquaintance. She took in and relished the compliments I gave her. She delighted in my interest in her work and activities but she never expressed any interest in what I do or think. If you would catch us together sometime, I would introduce her as a friend, but she will never be a lunch mate. She's not a friend I would call when I have something to share.

Some people have too much advice to offer, which stifles sharing. Once Job started honestly sharing his feelings, the comforting silence between him and his friends was broken. His friends felt like they had to defend God. They were strong, stern, and critical in their comments. Job did not experience the relief that can come from sharing, and we won't either unless we find persons willing to identify with us, listen to us, or give us that "I-know-how-you-feel" response.

Cheryl M. Smith, a pastor's wife, found just such a person, an older woman named Mary. Writing in her book *Kindling a Kindred Spirit*, Smith said, "Even though I liked Mary from the start, I didn't expect an older woman could become a close friend. But when the typical struggles of motherhood and the stresses of ministry threatened to break me, Mary seemed like a safe person to confide in. I am glad I did. In time, the sharing went both ways. Over countless cups of tea in her kitchen we shared laughter, wisdom and prayer. Through our friendship I found confidence to mother the children that God had given me, courage to trust God in new steps of faith and healing from my past."

5

Why Chicks Click

*W*hy did Mary specifically seek out Elizabeth after learning she was pregnant with God's child? Why didn't she stay in Nazareth where she could be near Joseph, her betrothed, and talk with him? They were the ones whose lives the baby's birth would immediately have an impact.

Maybe Mary told Joseph about her pregnancy before leaving for Elizabeth's. We don't know when he learned the news. We do know an angel of the Lord appeared to Joseph (A betrothed couple was legally bound to each other as a married couple would be.) Since he was thinking of divorcing Mary, does this mean he might have responded to her news with anger or disbelief? If he did, then maybe she had to get away, to talk to someone about Joseph's reaction.

On the other hand, Mary may have headed for Elizabeth's first before telling Joseph, because she left soon after Gabriel's announcement (Luke 1:39*a*). Maybe she needed to talk to a woman before she talked with Joseph. Full of mixed emotions and swirling thoughts, perhaps she needed to sort out what was happening before she had the courage to tell Joseph.

Either way, Mary wanted to talk with a woman, as many of us would. Women converse with males about many things, but sometimes, we prefer conversations with women. Why is that? What do we have in female conversations that we don't always have when talking with males? Why do chicks click?

People-interest

We click because much of our conversation revolves around relationships. Shelley E. Taylor writes in *The Tending Instinct: How Nurturing Is Essential for Who We Are and How We Live*, "Indeed, about two-thirds of conversational time goes to social matters: relationships, social events, likes and dislikes, and what other people are up to. No other topic—politics, work, or even sports—comes close."

Our interest in people starts early. From birth on, females are more tuned in to other people than men are. A female baby is more reactive and responsive to other human beings than a male infant. Baby girls smile more. They are more responsive to the cries of other babies in the nursery. They start crying along with another baby more readily than do newborn boys. Girl infants also babble more in response to the sight of a human face. Baby boys will react to an inanimate object as quickly as they will to a person.

This orientation toward people is reflected over and over in women across the lifespan. This difference in men and women is evident in the kinds of books we read, in the television programs we watch, in our value judgments, in the professions we choose, and *in what we talk about*.

This tendency to talk about people may be why women are often accused of being gossips, but studies show women don't gossip more than men. Both sexes are equal in engaging in hurtful talk and rumors about others. What people often label *female gossip* is simply the manifesting of interest in persons to a degree that is incomprehensible if not frustrating to a man. Men find it hard to understand the interest women have in people and the many details they include in their conversations—what she wore, how she looked, what he said, his stern look, the way she smiled, and so on. Women have a penchant for details, and that's another reason why we like to talk with each other. We want to include the details!

Penchant for details

Women's brains are constantly taking in and assimilating information from everything that's going on around them. It is as if we come equipped with special antennae—some kind of sensory organs that are always moving, circulating, picking up all sorts of information, details, and observations. We can absorb and later retrieve a good deal more peripheral information than men can. We can pick up minute things that are not normally observed by a male, and naturally, we like to include some of those details in our conversations.

When we want to include details in our conversations, other women are usually the ones who are more receptive. I learned this lesson long before I researched differences in men and women.

When our son Ben turned six, Bob and I invited children from his kindergarten class to a birthday party. Some of the children I had never met before. It was a beautiful spring day, so we played outside games, and Bob and I gave Ben a bicycle. Each child got to ride the bike. Bob was right with me, assisting me throughout the party. After it was over, I said to Bob, "Let's have a cup of coffee and talk about the party."

He said, "What's there to talk about?"

He walked away, went to the backyard shed, got out the lawn mower and started mowing the yard. The party was over; nothing more needed to be said or done.

There I was, needing to process the event, and no one to talk to. I couldn't stand it. I needed to talk about how the games went over, how the kids interacted with each other, what Ben's little playmates were like, whether Ben was pleased with the party, and so on. I called my neighbor Bettie, whom I mentioned in chapter 3, whose son had been at the party. I said, "Can you come over for coffee?" She did, and I talked about every facet of the party, and bless her heart, she was interested in every detail! Bettie smiled, nodded, and said *un-huh* and *oh* at all the right places.

I can only imagine the many details Mary and Elizabeth must have shared during their three months together. Elizabeth probably told Mary about Zechariah's not being able to speak when he got home from the temple in Jerusalem where he learned they were going to have a baby. She would tell Mary how Zechariah had to write her messages and how much patience that took on her part. She might mention where she was when he arrived home and how he looked when he walked in the door.

Mary would have told Elizabeth where she was when Gabriel appeared to her. She probably described how at first she was scared and then filled with wonderment. She would describe the trip alone through Samaria to Elizabeth's home in the Judean hills. Some of those details would have been picked up and replayed from time to time during their three months together.

I imagine Zechariah found excuses from time to time to work outside while the women talked. He might have even scratched his head, wondering how two women could cover so much territory and include so many details. He might have raised an eyebrow or two as he heard their laughter and their crying because women also like to share their feelings.

We click because we feel

God created both sexes to be emotional, feeling creatures, but women seem to be more in touch with their feelings and more able to articulate their feelings. This may be due to our culture. Boys have traditionally been taught to stifle their emotions, which could lead to not even acknowledging feelings. Our culture has agreed that it is all right for women to cry, but not for men. Girls and women who tend babies, nurture children, and serve as caretakers live close to their feelings, and this may make it easier for them to recognize their own feelings.

Or a woman's ability to be in touch with her feelings may be God-designed. In general, the human brain is composed of two hemispheres. The right hemisphere has to do with feelings and emotions; hence, men and women are emotional creatures; however, men have fewer connections between their hemispheres. The hemispheres of the female brain communicate in a less structured and more rapid way, possibly enabling women to be more in touch with their feelings.

With either explanation—or maybe one yet to be discovered—women as a whole are more in touch with their feelings. And because they are verbal specialists, something we noted in chapter 2, we're usually more adept at articulating our feelings than men are. Consequently, for women, sharing feelings becomes a large part of many conversations.

> Don't you know that Mary and Elizabeth couldn't have told their stories to each other without talking about their feelings?

Don't you know that Mary and Elizabeth couldn't have told their stories to each other without talking about their feelings?

- The joy of being selected by God
- The wonder of a child growing within her womb
- The thrill of experiencing a baby's first movement
- Their uneasiness at people's reactions, particularly Joseph's
- Their fears about the future

It would be hard for many women to talk about their experiences without sharing their feelings—feelings some men may not always understand or appreciate. Likewise, it is also important that we share our spiritual experiences.

Spiritual sharing

While God designed men and women to be spiritual creatures (Genesis 1:26a, 27), women appear to be more attuned to the spiritual. This may explain why Mary readily responded in beautiful submission to Gabriel's message whereas Elizabeth's husband questioned the angelic messenger. Both Mary and Zechariah received news of a special miraculous event that was to take place. Zechariah, whose wife was beyond childbearing age, disbelieved the message and was struck dumb as a result. Mary, a virgin, received the message with faith and submission.

Among the first to understand that Jesus must die for the world was Mary of Bethany, since she anointed Jesus for His burial (John 12:1–8). In the resurrection account, the women are the ones who expressed belief. Peter and the other apostles did not readily accept the news when they first heard it.

If you disagree with this premise—that women are more attune to the spiritual—then consider the choir membership in your church or the general attendance in your church. Do you have more men in those activities than woman? Does your church offer more Bible studies for women than they do men? Are men or women more involved in missions?

If you agree with this premise, then you can understand why women, who are verbal specialists, want to talk about spiritual experiences. When we do we want to share an experience with someone, who will understand and appreciate the experience—another woman.

Recently, in a speech to women, I told about an experience in which a single bloom on a hibiscus plant lifted my spirits. In fact, I even went so far as to say God prepared that bloom for me. The women listened and nodded in agreement; they understood! Afterwards, some of them shared with me their experiences of God speaking to them through nature.

I would never have told the hibiscus story at a gathering of men and women; I haven't even told my husband and sons, even though they are all Christians. I chose to tell it to women because I knew they would get it, and they did.

Mary may have needed to talk with a woman in those first moments after her supernatural experience. She needed someone who would not question the appearance of an angel or the unusual message he gave her. Perhaps Joseph did question the encounter and that was the reason he was ready to divorce her if God hadn't intervened. The one-sided conversation may have gone something like: *You say an angel visited you? You are pregnant but you haven't known another man? You say you are having God's child? You've got to be kidding!*

You have to admit Mary's story doesn't sound plausible, but Mary was there. Mary saw and heard and took in, so she went searching for someone who would believe her—another woman. For the same reason, we too may look for another woman to talk with about our spiritual experiences. We want a listener who will believe us and who will understand.

With more than two ears

Chicks click because we listen with our eyes as well as our ears. Women are adept at reading feelings in others. In "The More Social Sex" (*Newsweek*, May 10, 2004) Anna Kuchment writes, "Studies have shown consistently that women are better than men at reading and responding to subtle cues about mood and temperament." They see things men don't see such as intensities of facial expression like a frown or a raising of an eyebrow. They hear the emotional tone behind words, so they are better at sensing the difference between what people say and what they mean. Women are adept at picking up nuances that reveal another person's true feelings. They are also able to interpret social cues such as posture and gesture and quickly fit all sorts of peripheral information together and reach a conclusion such as "I know how you feel."

Another reason many women like to talk with other women is because of the feedback we receive as we speak. We can tell if we are being listened to as we take note of any affirming, encouraging signs coming our way. Women are more apt to give those signs in a conversation. They nod, ask questions, and signal interest by saying things such as *un-huh*, *yes*, or *go on*. They vocalize comfort and reassurance. They look at us and smile. In her article, Kuchment quotes Cambridge University psychologist Simon Baron-Cohen who said, "On average, women engage in more 'consistent' social smiling and 'maintained' eye contact than does the average man."

Another difference in the way men and women listen is when we want to talk in times of stress. This is a time when we instinctively feel a need to talk. We're not immediately concerned with finding solutions; instead, we are seeking relief by talking and being understood. At a time like this, a man may be only partially listening as a woman talks. He may be listening with part of his brain, but another part may be trying to figure out how he can help her. Many men want to act, to solve a woman's problem rather than simply listen. They want to assess what is bothering her and find a solution.

But we find relief in being able to express our worries, disappointments, and frustrations. If a listener relates to our frustration and disappointment, we feel understood and supported. If we feel we are being heard, our stress diminishes and often disappears. Once a woman shares her feelings, she feels better, which was what she was looking for in the first place.

By mentioning this difference, we're not saying that every woman is a good listener and every man wants to be a problem-solver. We are saying that this difference appears often enough to be true for many men and women. The question is: *Is it true in your life?* It is in mine.

After we moved, but before I found some lunch mates, I often found myself needing to talk. I'd say to Bob, "I need to talk." And, as we settled in comfortable chairs in the living room or across the table from each other in the dining room, I learned to preface our conversations with, "I need a listener and not a problem-solver." If I didn't Bob would immediately start offering solutions. Bob has a servant heart and wants to help, but at the moment, the help I needed was being "listened to."

Talking with men—husbands, boyfriends, brothers, fathers, co-workers, friends, and sons—will always be an important part of our lives. It's certainly a dynamic I wouldn't want to eliminate from mine. But on occasion, we women want to talk with someone who understands how we feel, who will hear us out as we describe details, and who will not be embarrassed by our feelings. We want a listener who won't rush to a solution without our getting to say what we need to say. We want someone who will look at us, who will smile, nod, and utter appropriate comments. We want someone to respond with "I know how you feel." That's why from time to time over the lifespan we want and often need to talk with other women. It's the way we are; it's a girl thing.

6

What? You, Too?

*I*f having another woman to talk with was important to Mary, why didn't she talk with her mother or to women in Nazareth? We don't know anything about her family, but in a town of the size of Nazareth, there would have been many women to share with. There would have been women her age giving birth to their first child. There would have been women a little older with several children under foot who could have given her lots of advice. There would have been older women, women Elizabeth's age with a wealth of wisdom to share, yet Mary chose to go to Elizabeth who lived miles away.[1]

In those days of no cars or trains, the trip must have been difficult and scary for a teenage girl. Did she walk? Did she ride a camel? A donkey? Did she encounter the scorn of the Samaritans? Nazareth was in Galilee, and Samaria separated Galilee from Judea. Good Jews wouldn't travel through Samaria because the animosity between the Samaritans and Jews was so strong. Mary would have gone through Samaria or around it to reach Elizabeth. Either way it would not have been an easy trip for a young woman in the beginning stages of pregnancy. Why was she so determined to see Elizabeth?

Finding a kindred spirit

Mary was a young woman and Elizabeth was old, past child-bearing age. Because of the age difference, many writers and speakers have suggested that Mary chose to go to Elizabeth because she was seeking a mentor. I don't think so! Elizabeth was not an experienced mother. I believe she went to Elizabeth because she knew Elizabeth would understand. In Elizabeth, she would find a kindred spirit.

Elizabeth would have an appreciation for the work of the supernatural in Mary's life. Mystery was involved in Mary's pregnancy. When Gabriel visited Mary, he said, *"Don't be afraid, Mary; God has been gracious to you. You will become pregnant and give birth to a son, and you will name him Jesus...The Holy Spirit will come on you, and God's power will rest upon you. For this reason the holy child will be called the Son of God"* (Luke 1:30–31,35). An angel appeared to Mary, but not everyone receives visits from angels not even in biblical times. Mary was a virgin, and this angel told her that she was going to have a baby! The angel was very specific that the baby would be a boy, that she was to call Him Jesus, and He would be the Son of God!

Now suppose she tried telling this to the women in her neighborhood. Who was going to believe her? They probably would have said something like: *You say an angel appeared to you and now you are going to have a baby? You say this is God's child? Yeah, sure, Mary.* Even Joseph, the man who loved her, thought of dissolving the relationship when he learned she was pregnant.

But Elizabeth would understand because God was working in her life as well. Her husband, Zechariah, had gone to the temple in Jerusalem to take his turn performing priestly duties. While he was there, the same angel that appeared to Mary appeared to him. He told Zechariah that he and Elizabeth would have a child, a special child who would prepare the way for the Messiah who would come.

Zechariah went home, and he and Elizabeth conceived a child. An old woman past childbearing years was going to have a baby because God acted! Her miracle baby was not as unusual as Mary's but still it was unusual.

Mary knew that Elizabeth would not call her crazy. Elizabeth could have said, *I know what you mean. Angels do appear. God works in mighty ways. Miracles do happen.*

As they marveled about God's working in their lives, they could have shared the glory. As they told their stories to each other—including the details!—and accepted their divine assignments; they could have shared the wonder of being chosen by God. Together they could have exclaimed, *You mean God chose us?*

As wonderful as it was to be chosen by God and to have supernatural experiences, it wasn't all bliss. What they faced also made them kindred spirits.

Talked about women

While both women found joy in being chosen by God and in experiencing miracles, their pregnancies wouldn't appear to others as something to take pride in. To the general public, their pregnancies would have been disgraceful, making them both "talked about" women.

Elizabeth's age would have caused people to talk. Having children was very important in her time, so when Elizabeth became pregnant, the Bible says the Lord took away her disgrace. Still she didn't leave the house for five months. Could it have been because she was afraid of the stares and whispers? People would have said, *Imagine having a child at her age! She'll never be able to keep up with a toddler!*

What people said about Elizabeth would have been nothing to compare with the accusations they would have made about Mary. At least, Elizabeth was married. Mary wasn't. She was unmarried and pregnant. Many would have considered her pregnancy as an unwed mother disgraceful.

Elizabeth worried about the future. *Will I live long enough to raise this baby?*

Mary also had concerns about the future as the mother of the Messiah. What exactly did that mean? What would be asked of her? Would she be capable of raising God's child?

Mary was probably a little shaky those last few miles before arriving at Elizabeth's house. Maybe some doubts were creeping in: *Did an angel really talk to me? Am I really going to have God's child? Will I be able to handle this awesome responsibility?* She needed reassurance and encouragement by the time she arrived at Elizabeth's home, and she was not disappointed.

When Elizabeth heard Mary's greeting, her baby moved within her (Luke 1:41). *"Elizabeth was filled with the Holy Spirit and said in a loud voice, 'You are the most blessed of all women, and blessed is the child you will bear!...How happy you are to believe that the Lord's message to you will come true!"* (Luke 1:41,45).

What encouragement for Mary! These are words that she wouldn't have wanted to miss, but she would have if she hadn't sought a woman who would understand—a woman who could truly say, "I know how you feel."

What friend can I call?

Even in the world of women, we don't share with all women. We're selective; we look for someone who will understand, which is why my mom wanted to call a friend when she learned her nephew's barn burned down (see chapter 4). Both our minds were filled with this tragic event, and I was there for her to talk with, but it wasn't enough. Why did she want to contact a friend?

I think Mom wanted someone her age, with her perspective. She felt the need to talk to a woman her age who would grieve with her over something like this happening to one of their adult children. She needed a kindred spirit. She needed someone who would grasp the magnitude of the situation in the same way she did. She needed someone who would understand.

This is a ministry that many of us need from other women.

"I need understanding from another woman who is in the same situation."

"I need someone about the same age, that has children about the same age, that relates to my lifestyle and things that I am going through."

"I need to know others are going through the same challenges that I am."

"I need to hear from other mothers that it's OK to want to give up, and it's OK to cry over spilled milk, especially on a clean floor. I need to know that they made it, and I will too."

"I've always bonded with women who are in 'the same boat' as I am and who can relate; i.e., balancing work/children/spouse, and also with women who seem to be on the same path as I am in their walk with Christ."

"We have become very good friends due to similar health problems."

"My best friend is 11 years older than me. We have so many things in common. I'm a pastor's wife, and her husband retired from 38 years as a pastor. She has been a real encouragement and support for me. It's hard to believe we aren't actually blood-related sisters."

Like Mary, we want someone who grasps our situation, who can relate to us, understand our challenges, and offer us reassurance.

When you become a mother, you want to be with other mothers. You want someone you can talk with about belly buttons, diapers, formula, and spit up. You learn from others, and it increases the joy of motherhood.

By the time your child is a teenager, you may still want other mothers to chat with. Only the topics of conversations change! The challenges are different now! For some the conversation may be more sobering than when you had babies, but still insightful.

Or maybe it is your marital status that causes you to seek other women in the same boat. You are single and you want to connect with other single women to discuss the ups and downs of dating. If you are married and your husband is hard to live with, you may want to be in a book study with other women. The book, naturally, will be about marriage!

Or maybe it is your work. You're a high school teacher and nothing gets your juices flowing like comparing notes with a fellow teacher. Even when you are discouraged, ready to throw in the towel, once you have dinner with another teacher, sharing your "war stories," you feel ready and eager to return to the classroom.

Or perhaps it is your take on the Christian life. You believe it should be taken seriously even though some have accused you of taking it too seriously. To keep trying to put into practice what Jesus taught, you find it helpful to meet with other women from time to time, women whose allegiance to Christ is similar to yours.

What a blessing it is to have someone like ourselves or in a situation like ours to talk with! I think Nina, a single missionary in the Philippines, summarized it best when she described what she misses most on the missions field. She said, "You might think it would be a dinner at Ponderosa, or hot water in the kitchen, or a bath tub. Not so! It is someone to share your thoughts and ideas with... It is just someone that you can relate to on your own particular spiritual and emotional level. There is something precious about having at least one other person who understands you and accepts you as you are—someone you can share your very heart with."

Understanding is precious

Finding and talking with someone who understands is reassuring. With some experiences we have, inner voices may be speaking messages such as: *You're silly to think this way;* or *You shouldn't be doing things this way;* or *You should be smarter.* Or you could simply be wondering if you are doing things the right way. Is this how a mother is supposed to behave? Is this what a pastor's wife does? When someone gives you back that "I-know-what-you-mean" response, those inner messages fade. If your listener "gets it," if she understands, then you realize you are not the only person who does these things or feels this way. You marvel, "What? You too? I thought I was the only one."

> Understanding is an avenue for power. There's a reason why mothers unite against drunk driving... to grieve the loss of a child, or women work on mission together.

Understanding is an avenue for power. There's a reason why mothers unite against drunk driving, why mothers band together to grieve the loss of a child, or why women on mission work together. Through conversation and connecting, they bring their emotions together, combine them and shape them into influential power. They can do this because they understand each.

Understanding takes away the loneliness that comes to us from time to time. Loneliness engulfs us when we are unable to sense that others are sharing, caring, supporting, or identifying with us. This loneliness could be the result of your environment—a true physical loneliness if you live in an isolated area. Or it could be loneliness that comes when there is no one like you around, something like Nina experienced on the missions field. Even if there are people around, even people like you, you may be lonely if you sense that others don't care to know you, wouldn't be empathetic to your concerns or have nothing in common with you. But when you encounter a spirit of understanding, the loneliness disappears.

As precious as it is to link up with someone in the same boat as we are, everyone we share with doesn't have to be *exactly* like us in order to receive a spirit of understanding. Naturally, we gravitate toward women just like us, and the conversations we have can be insightful, meaningful, stimulating, reassuring, and even rejuvenating. As beneficial as they are, though, we shouldn't hold back and wait to talk until we find someone in exactly the same situation. In some cases, we might have to wait a long time! And in the meantime, we would be missing the relief and refreshment that comes from talking to a woman who understands.

Knowing enough to understand

If we can find a woman who can understand the emotion, the gravity, the dynamics or the complexity of our situation, then we can still experience the power of connecting through conversation.

Often I'm put in the position of advising women who struggle with depression, not because I'm a counselor, which I'm not, but because I've written three books about depression. Usually our time together is limited, because the women often engage me in conversation after I have given a speech. I find many of them think their situation is unique. *There is no one who understands.* I encourage these women to look for a woman in their church who has been wounded at some time or other. I encourage them to look particularly for someone who has suffered a major loss and recovered to talk with.

One of the major causes of depression among women is loss. In dealing with her loss, if a woman learns from it, then she will be aware of how it affects a person. She will be conscious of the grief, the anger, and the hopelessness that is involved. She will have had the experience of dealing with those things herself; therefore, when she listens to others talk about their losses, she can nod her head and say, "I know how you feel," and it will be true. Even though her loss may be in the past or may be completely different from the speaker's, she understands the dynamics of recovering from loss.

To receive a spirit of understanding, our listener doesn't always have to be someone exactly like us, but she needs to be someone who can grasp our situation, see the dynamics involved, and have an appreciation for what we are experiencing.

Mary and Elizabeth weren't exactly the same—Mary was young and Elizabeth was old—but they could understand each other perspectives, because they had several things in common. Their commonalities connected them so they could draw strength from each other and experience the wonder of God together. It is common things that we want to be aware of as we look for women of understanding. The more we know about the lives of women, the more able we will be to identify these things. We'll have a basis for understanding each other. That's why in the next section, we are going to look at some aspects of a woman's life that will help us understand and find common ground for connecting.

---

[1] It is hard to figure the accurate distance between Mary's home and Elizabeth's since we don't know exactly where in the hill country of Judea Elizabeth lived. The distance could have been anywhere from 50 to 80 miles.

Part 2

Circle the Wagons, Girls

7

When I'm Stressed

h, an email message from Cathy! I'm always glad to see her name pop up on the computer screen; it's always interesting to find out what is happening with her. This time the subject line read, "Circle the wagons, girls; I'm heading for a crisis." What a creative way to express herself! The message was clear: she was under stress and she needed her friends.

The phrase *circle the wagons* comes from the days when pioneers moved into the western part of the United States by horse-drawn covered wagons. If they were in danger of being attacked, the pioneers pulled their wagons into a circle to protect themselves better. At night, when danger wasn't as obvious, but still lurking, they also formed a circle with their wagons.

Likewise, when we hit rough spots, we may need the surrounding support of other women. Talking with friends is especially helpful in dealing with stress, something we all encounter as we travel the road of life.

The stress we encounter

Women deal with all kinds of stress. Here are three broad categories.

1. *Stress from events that threaten our well being, burden our ability to function, or require substantial readjustment.* A divorce, a move, a job loss, a major failure, the birth of a baby, or a rejection might fit this category, although what's considered a stressful event varies from person to person. A situation that requires substantial readjustment for one person might be a slight inconvenience for another.

Naomi, whose story is told in the Old Testament book of Ruth, faced stress from events in her life: first, a famine in Bethlehem where she lived that prompted a move to Moab, and then the deaths of her husband and sons after she moved. The loss of a home, the loss of a mate, or the loss of a child affects a woman's ability to function each requires major readjustment.

2. *Chronic stress.* This is ongoing stress due to something you have to deal with day-in and day-out such as what a woman might experience in dealing with a rebellious teenager, caring for an emotionally disturbed child, assisting an invalid parent, working for a boss who consistently makes unrealistic demands, or managing ongoing financial problems. After her husband and sons died, Naomi and her daughter-in-law Ruth faced ongoing financial stress. This was not a time of equal employment for women or Social Security benefits for widows. In fact there were hardly any ways widows could provide for themselves. In Moab, where they were living, the challenge faced them. It accompanied them on their journey to Bethlehem, and it lingered with them after their return. Repeatedly Naomi and Ruth had to wonder, *How are we going to support ourselves?*

3. *Stress from overload.* For some women, the overload may be having too much to do, when the demands of their life exceed their ability to meet those demands. They are trying to keep too many balls circulating in the air because they can't say no or don't want to say no. Or they could be women forced by life situations to take on too many responsibilities. For example, a single parent who is trying to raise several children, hold down a job, and go to college may experience stress. In another situation, a woman who has to take on extra job duties because her company downsized could find herself in stress. She's overwhelmed by all she has to do.

Naomi's overload may not have had to do with too many responsibilities as much as it was due to the accumulation of all she had experienced. The heartache, the unwanted changes, the disappointed dreams, the loss of her husband, and the deaths of her sons stacked themselves up until their total weight made life hard to deal with. This may explain why Ruth had energy to tackle their survival challenge in Moab while Naomi seemed paralyzed, unable to act.

The word *stress* wasn't used to explain the tension we experience until the early 1930s. (Before this, it was called *life*!) Hans Selye, the world's premier stress researcher, introduced the notion of stress when he borrowed the word from physics to describe the body's responses to everything from flu viruses and cold temperatures to emotions such as fear or anger. In physics, stress is a force exerted when one body or body part presses on, pulls on, pushes against, or tends to compress or twist another body or body part. Don't those stress verbs *pressed on*, *pulled on*, *pushed against*, *compressed*, and *twisted* describe how you feel sometimes? What's a woman to do when she feels this way? Cathy would say, "circle the wagons," and scientists would say, she would stand and fight or flee as fast as possible.

Not fight or flight

Until recently, scientists generally believed that when people—men and women—experienced stress, a hormonal surge prompted the bodies to either stand and fight or flee as fast as possible. Now scientists are thinking otherwise about women. They are thinking we may have a larger behavioral range than just fight or flight. Important studies at both the Los Angeles and Irvine branches of the University of California suggest that women respond to stress by tending to their children and gathering with women.

Researchers are currently focusing on two kinds of hormones—oxytocin and endogenous opiods—that are associated with feelings of relaxation and nurturing. Both are released when women are lactating. The hormones help women bond emotionally to their newborns. And some experts believe that the same hormones may help us bond as women. Psychologist Larry Jamner of the University of California, Irvine, tested this hypothesis. He gave opioid-blocking agents to college students—22 men and 29 women—and watched them for 3 days. The men's social behavior showed no difference, but the women's behavior changed dramatically. The women spent more time alone and called their friends less often. When they did socialize, the women reported that the gatherings were less pleasant than usual.

When oxytocin is released as part of a stress response, it shields the fight or flight response and encourages a woman to tend children and to gather with other women. When she actually engages in tending and befriending, more oxytocin is released, which further counters stress and produces a calming effect. This calming response does not occur in men. Men produce high levels of testosterone when they're under stress, which reduces the effects of oxytocin. Estrogen enhances oxytocin.

What prompted researchers to consider that perhaps women might respond differently to stress than men was an observation in their lab. When the women who worked in the lab were stressed, they came in, cleaned the lab, had coffee, and bonded. When the male scientists were stressed, they holed up somewhere by themselves. This is a pattern that John Gray recognized years earlier and wrote about in his book *Men Are from Mars, Women Are from Venus*. Men want to go off in a cave to deal with their stress and women want to talk.

Talk: the great stress reliever

According to Gray, when a woman is stressed she instinctively feels a need to talk about her feelings and all the possible problems associated with her stress. He said that she finds relief through talking in great detail. Gradually, if she feels she is being listened to, her tension diminishes and sometimes disappears altogether. For a woman, talking is a natural and healthy antidote to stress.

Talking can change a woman's focus. Stress can be mentally and emotionally absorbing, commanding a woman's complete attention. Once a woman feels listened to she stops dwelling so much on her problems and becomes more positive.

If a woman can talk about the stress that is weighing her down, her load will lighten. As we noted in an earlier chapter, a shared load is a lighter load.

Talking provides an emotional release. With stress, we can experience many different emotions. We may be anxious, worried, ashamed, angry, or depressed, and talking about those feelings—even venting—diminishes their power and helps us gain control over them.

When Andrew Solomon, the author of *The Noonday Demon: An Atlas of Depression*, is asked by people how best to treat depression, he tells them to talk about it. He encourages them "not to work themselves up into hysteria about it, but simply to keep articulating their feelings. Talk about it with family if they'll listen. Talk about it with friends. Talk about it with a therapist." He echoes the thoughts of Shakespeare's Hamlet, we "unpack our hearts with words."

Naomi certainly didn't hesitate to unpack her heart. When she and Ruth arrived in Bethlehem, Naomi's hometown, her old friends were happy to see her. *"The women exclaimed, 'Can this be Naomi?'"* (Ruth 1:19 NIV).

"'Don't call me Naomi [pleasant],' she told them. 'Call me Mara [bitter], because the Almighty has made my life very bitter. I went away full, but the Lord *has brought me back empty. Why call me Naomi? The Lord has afflicted me; the Almighty has brought misfortune upon me'"* (Ruth 1:20–21 NIV).

Through unpacking her heart, a woman gains relief, energy, and help for dealing with her stress. She may also gain more insight too. Some of the relief gained by Naomi by venting may have helped her think more clearly so she could eventually recognize a solution to her and Ruth's dilemma. It was in a conversation with Ruth that Naomi had a burst of inspiration about a possible solution.

Talk: an eye-opener

Ruth was providing food for herself and her mother-in-law by gathering grain in the fields that were owned by a man named Boaz. When she took the grain home, Naomi noticed what a large amount the young woman had gathered. She asked Ruth, *"Where did you gather all this grain today? Whose field have you been working in? May God bless the man who took an interest in you!"* (Ruth 2:19).

Did you notice the exclamation mark? Naomi's stress was lifting; her mood was changing as was her view of God.

Ruth told Naomi that she had been working in a field belonging to Boaz. Naomi's mood brightened even more, and the wheels of her mind started turning in a positive direction. Boaz was a relative, and perhaps he was the answer to their problem of survival. Her view of the future improved.

Through talking, as we externalize our problems, we can get a clearer picture and possibly see solutions. Stress consists of our inner reaction to events and demands, and through talking we can change our inner reactions and gain hope and insight about our situation.

In addition, we will probably also gain the support of the women we talk with about our stress. It may not be anything she particularly does, but in how she listens, in her attitude, in her mannerisms, in her prayers, in her comments, and in her checking back with you later, you will feel supported. She may actually rally the troops and come to your material aid. She might take the children for a while to give you a break, do your laundry to give you some much needed time, or organize a casserole brigade with meals being brought in every night for a week. In these ways, you will feel shored up and strengthened for what you have to face.

Talking and having someone to listen to us refreshes and renews us when dealing with stressful events, ongoing stress, or the heaviness of stress. It has long-term benefits as well. Study after study has found that social ties reduce our risk of disease, and having friends help us live longer. Women with good friends are blessed with less stress, and when they do encounter stress they have someone to turn to and to talk with. Can we do without them? Forty-three-year-old Mary, married with children, says she can't. In her survey she wrote, *"Sometimes I think I wouldn't survive if I didn't have my girlfriends to minister and nurture, or for them to minister or nurture me. It's great having best friends there for me."*

You'll notice Mary said *friends*. For dealing with stress, we need friends. If we only have one friend, we might be tempted to depend on her to hear all our woes. That's a good way to end a friendship! Or we might find one friend might not understand a particular tension we are experiencing. To get relief or gain support, we may need friends who understand various facets of our lives. Also, what happens if you have only one friend and she's unavailable when you need to talk?

There are times too when like Cathy, we want a circle of friends to help us deal with stress. We want to be surrounded by love; we want to be protected and supported on all sides, or we just might like getting various perspectives on our situation.

The circle

Cathy may not have realized when she typed the words *circle the wagons, girls* the importance of the word *circle*. Although we don't use the word much, the concept is important. When we talk and we vent, we often sit around tables with something to do or something to eat in our midst. Together, we laugh and we cry. We turn to such gatherings to share our feelings, to feel better about ourselves and life, and to seek support and solutions. What we end up with are healthier, happier lives.

To have this, some of us gather in circles on a regular basis. It may be a group of quilters sitting in someone's family room with our works in progress spread out before us. It may be a book club or a Bible study or a garden club. It may be a scrapbooking group where chatter takes place as scissors cut and glue is spread.

Jane Johnson Struck, writing in "Building Deep Connections," (*Today's Christian Woman*, March/April 2002), tells about Barbara Jenkins who in her own way said, "Circle the wagons, girls." After her husband walked out on her, and one of her children was caught up in alcohol and drugs, Barbara Jenkins felt her world had turned upside down.

Jenkins saw in the Bible how Jesus changed the world with 12 disciples and realized she could benefit from having a trusted circle of 11 other friends to help her carry burdens. "When she shared the idea with a few women, they recommended others who were searching for such a connection," says Struck. "Before long, a diverse mix of 11 women had accepted Barbara's invitation." They met once a week, grounding their meetings in biblical truth, talking and supporting one another.

I would get lost in a group of 12—that's too big of a circle for me! I'm not shy, but my personality is such that I am reluctant to talk about my stress in a very large group. I still like and often need a circle, though, just a smaller one.

Interestingly, you may not go to a group for a conscious connection, for conversation or therapy! You may say you are going to learn how to cook, to study the Bible, to gain knowledge, but in the interaction (the talk!) that takes place, your load is lightened, your insight increased, and your hope level raised as you connect.

As we travel life's highway, navigating its twists and turns, we're tempted to think—and sometimes we do think—that we are the only ones who have to endure stress. You look at the well-manicured, every-hair-in-place woman and think, *She would never understand how harried things get in my life.* As your children scuffle in the pew, you look at the well behaved children of the woman sitting across the aisle, and think, *I bet she never gets impatient with her children.* In a weak moment, when you are really hungry, you buy a donut at the bakery, and a very slender friend spots you and stops to say hi. Inwardly you groan and think, *She probably doesn't even know the meaning of the word temptation.*

Alone with ourselves, we feel separated from others. Our inner voice says: *No one has the troubles I do. No one else feels the way I do.* But when we join a circle of women where we talk and interact, the barriers come done. The result is stress relief and a sense of solidarity, a "we're-in-this-together" kind of spirit.

We will never have a life without stress, but we can have friends and conversation to deal with the stress as long as we're willing to say, "Circle the wagons, girls; I need to talk."

8

When I Need a Sounding Board

*A*t various times in life, all women encounter change. Sometimes it comes suddenly and unexpectedly as it did for Mary and Naomi. I can't imagine Mary predicting ahead of time that she was going to be pregnant by God's Spirit. She probably dreamed of having children "someday" after she and Joseph were married. With Gabriel's announcement, her life abruptly changed. Naomi didn't expect the deaths of her sons; parents are not supposed to outlive their children.

Sometimes change is expected as it looms on the horizon. It may even be something you're anticipating, even looking forward to. You're in college, and you daydream about how your life will change once you graduate. You're in love, and you expect your life will be very different once you get married.

On the other hand, change could be on the horizon, and not something you are looking forward to. You like having children at home, and you don't want your nest to empty. You love your job and you never want to retire.

Some changes are clearly marked with a specific event such as a death, a marriage, an accident, a job termination, or a tornado. In other words, the change is obvious; other people can recognize it happening. Some changes, though, take place within, or may start within and later become visible to others. Something stirs inside you, upsetting your pattern of life and heralding the consideration of a new pattern. Images of another life beckon you, or other possibilities become attractive. God may be calling you to a new place of service, a new task, or a new direction.

In our lives, we have expected and unexpected changes. We encounter changes we want and some we don't. We have changes that are obvious and others that are not so obvious. All of these, though, have their particular challenges, and to deal with them, we may need some girl talk. Here are some reasons why.

To deal with emotions

All kinds of emotions accompany change, and many of those will need to be expressed to move forward successfully. In the last chapter, we learned the importance of "unpacking" our feelings to deal with stress. Change is certainly stressful, involving many adjustments. Even positive change is stressful. As plans are made, emotions may be running high.

For changes we don't want to make, the emotions may have to do with what we are leaving behind or giving up. One in particular is grief, because something is being given up. Things will no longer be the same. We may grieve over what was lost. To be able to share this grief with someone reduces the intensity of the grief and comforts us.

Depression and anger may be part of the picture, particularly if the change is something you feel you had no choice about. Even though Georgia (not her real name) filed for divorce, she was filled with rage at being put in the position of having to seek one. Her husband was abusive; her life and the lives of her children were in danger. Her husband refused to get help. She poured out the rage to her friend Barbara.

"I had to leave," she sobbed. "He was hurting me. He was hurting my kids. Do you understand?"

Barbara nodded her head. She did understand. She said, "It must have been terrible." Unpacking Georgia's emotions took many conversations. Sometimes Barbara responded with a hug; other times she would just sit with her friend. Often she would pray with her. But always she would listen. Georgia says, "Because of Barbara, I was able to get through the pain."

Emotions may have to do with what we are facing such as fear of the future. Cindy was afraid after her husband asked for a divorce. In her survey reply, she wrote, "I am not happy. I loved being married, but obviously my ex-spouse didn't. I love my children more than life, but I am terribly lonely and afraid of being alone for the rest of my life."

Sometimes we can't even name what we are feeling, but a good listener can help us. By letting us talk things out ("unpack our hearts"), we can untangle our negative emotions and identify how we really feel.

Of course, positive emotions also accompany some changes. You become engaged and you want to shout the news to the world. Instead, you settle for calling your friends. You find out you're pregnant, and like Mary, you have to find someone to tell, to share in the happiness with you. Sharing, as we learned in chapter 4, multiples the joy.

To sort out our confusion

While talking with an understanding person can help us deal with our emotions, it can also help us sort out our confusion. With some changes, especially those that are unexpected and disruptive, a period of confusion and disorientation may follow. A tornado sweeps through your area and almost destroys your home. You may be so overwhelmed by the loss that you don't know where to start rebuilding your house or your life. The insurance papers you need to fill out are incomprehensible. You have no idea what community resources are available to help you. Having a friend who can think this through with you can be an enormous help.

Changes that begin within may cause a person to go through an "in between time," when she is not who she was and not who she will be. You may need a listening ear to help you figure out just what God is saying to you or what is prompting you to contemplate a new life.

Sometimes the change you are being forced to make—or even ones you want to make—don't have a clear path to follow at least, not at first. You know something must be done, but what's the first step? This, too, can be figured out by talking, maybe having someone help you answer questions such as: *What do I do now?*; *How am I going to cope?*; and *What is really transpiring here?* It is amazing how much clearer our path becomes if we can talk with someone who will really listen. We'll be able to see the change for what it is, understand some of the dynamics involved, and eventually see what steps to take.

As we share with a woman who understands, we come to a clearer understanding of ourselves (Proverbs 20:5) or of our situation. There's something about getting the thoughts out in the open and talking about them that improves our vision. We see things in a better light.

To examine possibilities

As our vision improves, we'll want to evaluate our situation. Are there other people involved? How will the change affect them and our relationships with them? If the situation is destructive, we can assess what can be salvaged and what choices we have. Even if there doesn't seem like there are any choices, there are. If nothing else, we have a choice about what our attitude will be. Is it: "I can't go through with this" or "I'm going to make the best of this situation"?

I realize most of us don't sit down with our friends and say, "What can I salvage?" or "What are my choices?" but those questions may be answered in unhurried conversations. Over lunch or several lunches, we can "hear" our attitude when we verbally ponder our situation. With our penchant for details, we can note what we have to work with as we talk. And as we do, something transpires. Our hope level rises. Even when the circumstances are totally distasteful, we can begin to see how we can grow and gain from the experience. We can begin to see possibilities for happiness when earlier the landscape looked barren and bleak.

When change is desirable, conversations can be creative, percolating talks where possibilities are explored. This can be an exciting, stimulating process.

Once we see possibilities—whether the change is desirable or undesirable, we can identify specific alternatives, weigh them, and decide on the best course of action. Here again, we may need some help from our friends. After we've "unpacked our hearts," we need "refilled hearts." We need hearts filled with decisiveness, courage, and determination.

Moving forward

You can express your emotions, sort out your confusion, examine possibilities, and still not successfully navigate change. You have to move forward and embrace the future. This takes decisiveness, courage, and determination.

Among those alternatives you identified, one has to be selected in order to move forward. You can't do them all! Some women may find it hard to be decisive because they want too much to please others; they're afraid of not pleasing God; or they are afraid of failing. They keep hesitating, making a decision because they worry: *What if I make the wrong decision? What if it doesn't work out? What if I am wrong? Yikes, what if I fail? What if I won't be happy?*

Not only must a woman be decisive in navigating change, she must be determined. The past, the way things were, has a magnetic pull that holds a woman back. That's one reason you find it hard to keep going as you let go of one way of being and discover a new way of being. Here's where you need to be determined.

But even on the upswing, after you have made the decision, adjustments are still necessary. Your life is taking a new direction, and adjustments are required. They can be discouraging. You never expected it to be so hard. You never expected to face so many hurdles. Risks may be involved, and you may be scared about taking those risks.

But the women we talk with can be our cheerleaders. They can urge us on. In unhurried, conversational times together, our friends can inject hope and courage into us. Dealing with troubling emotions and confusion may erode our human spirit, leaving us without the determination to move forward, but having a friend or two who will encourage us will boost our spirits.

A friend may encourage you with what she says. When she says such words as *Hang in there; Don't give up; You made the right decision; God will get you through this* you are encouraged. As Proverbs 15:23 says, *"how good is a timely word!"* (NIV). It is indeed.

She may encourage you with her smile, her presence, or a "thumbs up," but most of all, she will encourage you with her listening ear. Every woman dealing with change needs a sounding board. She needs a listener who will help her gain insight into her situation, help her untangle her emotions, sort out her thoughts, find solutions, and gain courage.

Some words of caution

As valuable as listening is, this doesn't mean we should expect our friends to be professional counselors or therapists. Don't expect them to always say the right thing or ask probing questions as we might expect of a professional. Even if our friends don't say the right thing, they help simply by listening.

I first learned the value of listening when I was thinking about making a change. Something was stirring inside me, making me wonder if I should change from being a curriculum writer to being a book writer. Curriculum writing was steady; book writing would be haphazard even if I could get a contract. I had no guarantee that I would. As I contemplated this possible change, I wondered: *Is God speaking to me, or is this Brenda speaking?* After having been a leader of prayer groups, I wanted to express myself on prayer but there were already many books on prayer available. *What would I have to say that would be unique or helpful?*

During this time of consideration, we had a house guest, a woman in her late 70s who knew very little about writing and publishing. Ramona and I had been friends for several years because she needed a daughter and I coveted her grandmotherly interest in my children. During this visit, we mostly talked about her needs, her feelings, and her travels. After several days, we had exhausted the normal topics of conversation. Silence rose up between us like a great boulder one afternoon when the children were napping. To deal with the awkwardness of the silence, I started talking. She had been in some of the prayer groups that I had led, so I talked about some of our experiences and what I had learned. I also mentioned the possibility of writing a book.

> In that unhurried time together she gave me great eye contact, smiled, and nodded her head. She listened, and as I talked it became clear to me that God was calling me to write a book.

Ramona didn't know enough to ask leading questions, but in that unhurried time together she gave me great eye contact, smiled, and nodded her head. She listened, and as I talked it became clear to me that God was calling me to write a book. I also figured out that it would be a question-and-answer book on prayer. I would write about the questions that came up repeatedly in our prayer groups. Resolve rose in me as I talked; I determined I would do it. Her listening encouraged me to change, and the result was my first book called *Prayerfully Yours.*

To have someone really listen to us—whether a professional or a nonprofessional—comforts us, raises our hope level, improves our vision, nourishes our spirit, and gives us courage to move forward.

This is not to say that talking and listening is our only tool for dealing with change. For some changes that we navigate, we may need to see a member of the clergy or a mental health professional. We may prefer an in-depth Bible study or to read a self-help book. We may want to write in a journal, pray the Scriptures, or any of a number of other things.

God has blessed us with many resources we can use for navigating change; it is not a matter of one being more important than the others or superior to the others. It is a matter of being blessed with multiple resources to select from. We can select the ones that fit our situation and that suit us. For many women, what suits us—what comes naturally—is to navigate change by connecting and conversing. This is how we can gain understanding, insight, and encouragement.

9

When Handling Life's Stages

Not everyone travels the same yellow brick road of life. There's much variety in how we live our lives, and yet the yellow brick road has some predictable stops along the way—what specialists in adult development call *stages*. The dividing lines between stages are fuzzy; that is, every one doesn't exit or enter at the same chronological age. Each stage is not marked by a number as much as it is by a shift in thinking and emphases as women develop and change.

Naturally, we gravitate toward women who are in the same stage, but our lives can also be enriched by conversations and interactions with women who are in a different stage. Knowledge of the various stages of a woman's life can help us connect. Each stage contains new challenges, new responsibilities, and new joys. If we develop an awareness of what each stage is about, we'll improve our ability to connect through conversation. We can help each other meet life's challenges, handle its responsibilities, and increase our joy by talking and listening with understanding.

The exploratory stage

There's not an audience watching like you are on a theater stage, but you may feel like you are being watched when you step out on the first stage of adult development. This stage occurs when you are in your late teens and early 20s when you may feel like the world is watching to see what you are going to do!

During this exploratory time, a woman is in the process of separating from her family of origin and becoming an independent, autonomous adult. It is a time of freedom and hopefulness as she moves away from all that has defined her in the past. With her options wide open, she may feel carefree and blessed as she looks toward the future with great hope, thinking about what she wants to be when she "grows up." *What career path will she choose? Will she get married? Will she stay single? Will she have children?*

Eventually, though, choices must be made, and this can be stressful. *What if you make the wrong choice? What if you make a choice, then don't like the result and wish you had chosen otherwise?* Some do and have to make more choices, almost as if they are trying on different roles to play on the stage of human development, until they find the one that fits. This may be hard for your audience to understand, especially your parents! *When is that girl going to settle down and stay with something?*

And, eventually, you may realize you are not as free as you thought. You want a certain kind of job, and your grades aren't good enough to get you admitted to college. You really want to be a wife and mother but you seldom date.

It is also complicated. Once a choice is made, more choices may follow. For example, choosing marriage means choosing between marriage with children or marriage without children. Choosing to have children means more questions. *When shall we start a family? How many children will we have?*

Lisa, age 22 and single, expressed this stage's frustration well when she wrote: "I grapple with my desire to have fun and...my sense of responsibility. I ask questions like: Am I in the right career? Will others respect me? How do I get where I want to go? What role will my dreams play in the future? Will I get married? Will I be a good mom and wife? Will I make an impact for God? What if I mess up? What if what I want is not what God wants? What if I make a mistake? Is it OK to make mistakes?"

A woman in the exploratory stage of adulthood is filled with questions, and consequently, she needs to talk. She needs listeners who will let her verbally explore her options, who will take her concerns seriously, who will let her look at the ins and outs of various possibilities, and who will realize how important this process is. Late at night in the dorm or over coffee at Starbuck's, much time may be spent hashing and rehashing her options with others in the same situation.

> Late at night in the dorm or over coffee at Starbuck's, much time may be spent hashing and rehashing her options with others in the same condition.

In this time of uncertainty, when you could make poor choices, but hope you don't, you need friends to believe in you. As Kathleen said: "I need a type of nurturing that says: *Hey, you're OK! I believe in you.*" Basically, you need someone to see you not as you are, but as you want to be.

Because of the need to be encouraged and to feel supported, women in this stage often feel a special pull toward women who have "already been there." In her survey, Melissa, who is 20, wrote: "It's nice to have someone older that you can share feelings and struggles with. Knowing they have been where I am and then are where they are now is encouraging. It helps me believe things will work out."

When the exploration loses its urgency, your questions are answered, your priority shifts to building a life, and you are no longer dependent on your parents, then you are in life's next stage—the stage where you show the world that you have grown up.

Are we grown up yet?

The next stage is young adulthood. I call this stage "the earnest years" as you try to secure a niche in your work, your community, your family and/or your church. You want to prove to your parents and to the world that you can do it.

Women in this stage want to be affirmed by others for accomplishments and personal qualities important to them. They want to be seen as competent.

A wife wants her husband to find her attractive and interesting—a competent partner in their joint enterprise.

A mother wants to earn respect and admiration for her maternal labors. She may worry that what she does now in raising her children will be reflected on later as wrong. She very much wants to do it right.

A woman whose occupation is important to her—or who is career focused—wants to be affirmed as a worker and to speak increasingly with her own voice in the work place.

A woman who views church or ministry as important may seek places of leadership and become more vocal about her faith. She's earnest about being a good Christian.

All of these pursuits can be rewarding, so under reasonably favorable conditions, this is a richly satisfying time. The woman who pursues a career has a great opportunity for personal development and recognition. Motherhood brings with it its own set of rewards. She can experience the joy and fulfillment that comes with leadership.

This stage is one of productivity. This doesn't mean all women in this stage are producing the same thing. Some are producing careers; others are producing products; some are making a niche in society; and many are producing children. Whereas earlier the urgency was to explore, now the urgency is to build. During this stage, high energy and effort are put into making a life, maintaining it, and enhancing it as women try hard to please bosses, coworkers, family members, and fellow Christians.

In this stage of competence, rewards, and productivity, you would think a woman might not need friends, but she does. She needs to check in with them and learn from them as she wonders, *Am I doing it right?* She needs women in the same place to compare notes with and ask, *How am I doing?*

At the same time, a young adult woman also needs friends who will allow her to "let her hair down" from time to time, people who will accept her as she is and to allow her to ease up on her effort, at least temporarily. Over lunch, sharing soup and salad, she can vent about her boss and know her image with her friend won't be affected in any way. On a park bench, with coffee and bagel in hand, she can express anger at her husband or her frustrations as a parent, knowing she will be accepted, warts and all.

While this kind of "letting-your-hair-down" conversation is beneficial to the young adult woman, whether she is talking with someone in her stage, the previous stage, or an older woman, it is not easy to achieve. For women in this stage, there is never enough time to achieve all she wants to achieve or to talk with friends about her frustrations.

> *"Being a working mother, my challenge is definitely time. If I didn't work (and it's pretty much a necessity that I do…my husband is a teacher at a Christian school), I feel that I would have the time to do laundry, go grocery shopping, clean the house, etc., in a much less hustle-bustle approach."* Gale, 38, married with children

"It is hard to be a married, full-time working parent! There are so many things I would like to be involved in, but can't because there are so many other obligations!" Janise, 35, married with children

"I can't sit back and relax and enjoy things. I feel pressured to make sure everything is done for everyone, household duties, church obligations, etc." Sammie, 35, married with children

"I'm a stay at home Mom...I would love to have time for myself, for my friends, for my husband, for my church, etc., but I also have to make difficult choices about time management. Some days all I do is survive all the battles my kids have. Some days I can't remember if I ate or if the kids ate. I also wonder when my last shower was." Jana, 32, married with children

Eventually, though, there is time...not all the time in the world, but more time than she had. Motherhood responsibilities wind down. The job becomes routine. The earnestness of the proving years wanes. You no longer feel so compelled to work hard to please others or to be perfect. As one respondent described it, "The drive in me has slowed down." After all the effort young adults put into building a life, it is interesting that some of them may want to rebuild when they reach middle adulthood.

When the questions return

Women who pursued careers may now enjoy a measure of respect for their competency and expertise. They have a sense of finally having arrived. Those who focused on community or church work may now feel a sense of accomplishment and competency. Mothers take pride in how their children turned out or even in how they themselves turned out! Enjoying a stronger sense of self than they may have known before, they may begin to wonder: *What else is out there? What will I do with the rest of my life?* As one respondent wrote, "I'm enjoying the effects of experience, the equanimity that comes from having seen or done it before. It's great to know how to do things, where things are, what one likes, yet still be young enough to be willing—and able—to try something new."

The midlife woman believes that she can continue to evolve and is no longer so consumed by her roles. She may want to try out a new role, make a job change, or go from the corporate world to the volunteer world or from the volunteer world to the corporate world! She may want to start investing herself in other people and serving their needs. Adult developmental specialists call this *generativity*. This is when you voluntarily obligate yourself to care for and about others in a broader sense than what you did in the past, and you find personal fulfillment in doing so.

Once your goals may have been directed toward success, productivity, and making it in the adult world, they now may revolve around cultivating relationships with younger people, finding joy in conversations with them, and acting as a mentor or being a friend. Beverly is a middle-aged woman with health problems who invests in a younger woman. She said, "I love being a part of Tammy's life and having her children come by and give me a hug. It's great to see her mature in the Lord and become the wonderful person God created her to be. This relationship helps me think back to the joys I had in child rearing and puts some of my difficulties in perspective."

The freedom of some women in midlife to choose what they will do next may be hampered by family matters. What will she do about her aging parents? What will she do about her adult children who still need her or who moved back home? In some cases, what will she do about her grandchildren? For some, her increased responsibilities may include all three—aging parents, problem children, and caring for grandchildren. This is not to say there aren't solutions. There are, but it is to say while some midlife women have many options to consider; others may be limited because of their relationships.

At the same time, midlife women experience hormonal changes as their bodies prepare for and experience menopause. Their metabolic activity declines. They may begin having health problems as the consequences of past lifestyles or health habits catch up with them. As their stamina diminishes, it is easy to begin to think they have no choices. Laura who is 59 wrote, "It's unsettling to realize that the end is closing in, to see friends turning into 'old people,' who are getting old-people limits and illnesses, who will soon be dying. It's disquieting to realize that not everything is still possible, like it was for so many years; that there are places I'll never be able to visit and things I won't be able to do."

But here is where friends are helpful. Girl talk can lighten the load of worries over jobs, children, parents, change, aging, health, and hurdles.

"I need girl talk about children, grandparenting, middle life crisis, empty nest, needs of our husband, and our husbands as head of the household." Connie, 43, married with children

"I need a group that discusses women growing older and the physical changes they go through." Judy, 45, married with children

"I need to be encouraged that aging is an adventure to live through, not something to dread!" Jill, 49, married with children

Once the question *What will I do with the rest of my life?* is answered—once peace is made with your options—life will plateau for a while as new interests and goals are pursued and responsibilities are handled. Life's next stage is later adulthood. It is hard to pinpoint exactly when this stage begins. This may be because few people want to enter this stage! But fortunately there are girlfriends on the other side who are saying, "Come on over; it is not what you think."

Have I made an impact?

Retirement may be the marker for some that they are leaving middle adulthood and entering later adulthood, but that may occur long before you start thinking of yourself as old. Some people retire in their 50s, but even people who retire at 65 or 67 may not think of themselves in their later years, especially if they are healthy. Middle adulthood can go on a long time!

Later adulthood could also be defined as a time of physical challenges just as Laura (quoted above) feared it would be when health care and physical limitations become all encompassing and options are limited. But more than likely, later adulthood will arrive when you start chewing on the question, *Have I made an impact?*

To feel content and at peace with the meaning of life is a developmental task of the later years. Self-evaluation and much thought about one's life go into making peace with the past. This is why many older people have a strong tendency to reminisce as they relieve past experiences; they are doing a mental life review: *How did I get here? Has my life had value for others and me? Were the benefits to others and me worth the struggle? Am I leaving the world a better place?*

A person must be able to answer such questions in order to complete the life cycle with a sense of satisfaction and completeness. When women take a broad view of life—something they might not have been able to do in busier times when they were actively running society, building careers, and raising children—they can see what part they played or can still play in the drama of life. They can look back—and look forward—with a sense of integrity rather than despair.

Younger women can help older women answer the question, *Have I made an impact?* They can ask older women about their past, helping them discover their life's worth. They can ask them about their Christian experiences, how they raised their children, what their secrets to a long marriage were, and what kind of work they did.

Younger women can also help older women feel needed, something important because they find joy in being able to help to others. Titus 2:3–5 instructs older women to teach younger women. Often when I speak about this passage to female audiences, I remind them that there is mandate in the passage for younger women as well. It is not specifically stated, but it is implied. The older women can't teach unless younger women are willing to learn from them. Older women can't share their wisdom unless younger women want to receive it.

Younger women, though, can't understand aches and dizzy spells or the importance of staying in your own home, so older women, like women in the other stages, seek listeners who understand. Consequently, they talk among themselves about aging, things younger people might find awkward or foreign; and they don't wince at the mention of death. They get a kick out of little things, finding a bargain, going to lunch, and just talking with each other. Together, they make light about their memory losses, weight, and wrinkles. Laughing about the ups and downs of life reduces their stress, provides perspective, increases energy, and generally makes women feel better. In their playfulness, they often hang out in ensembles like they did as adolescents. Girl talk continues!

This camaraderie is particularly true of elderly widows, something important for all of us to keep in mind as many women outlive their husbands. Some sources say there are five times as many widows as widowers. Another says elderly women outnumber elderly men three to two. One said 11 out of 12 older adults are women. You get the picture: older adulthood is a female terrain. Those women who function best after the loss of their spouse and whose lives remained vital are those who have close friends and confidantes.

The "girl thing" of needing to talk and to connect continues through the various stages of life. Throughout the adult woman's life span—the exploratory years, the young adult years, the middle years, and the later years, the power of conversation is a sustaining force.

10

When We're Better Together

V ery early on the Sunday morning after Jesus died on Friday, some of His friends went to the tomb where His body had been placed (Mark 16:1–2). They were women who were taking spices to anoint Jesus's body. They went even though they had no idea how they would open the tomb. The women knew that it was beyond their strength to move the large stone that marked the tomb's entry, but they went anyway. As they walked, they talked among themselves about how they might get the tomb opened (Mark 16:3).

This picture of these determined women replays itself over and over in my mind, reminding me of the strength and courage women have when we work together. When we have a big job to do, when we want to minister together, when we want to do missions, when we want to accomplish a goal, many of us count on camaraderie and conversations with other women to get the work done.

When there's work to be done

You may be surprised to see friendship being associated with work. We don't usually link these two together, but much of life is about work. We spend many hours on the job. From part-time to full-time to over-time, we spend 20 to 60 hours or more a week working. In those hours, many of us have projects to complete or goals to reach.

Many of us want to accomplish things outside of our jobs that involve work, when we exert physical or mental effort or emotional energy to produce something or to achieve change. You may be motivated to seek change at your children's school, get a playground built in your neighborhood or run for public office. Or you may want to do something on a personal level that requires "elbow grease;" it stems from your desire to get something done.

Much of what God calls us to do involves work. If you have planned a missions trip, organized dinners for volunteers, coordinated a women's retreat, or directed Vacation Bible School, you know what I mean!

In all of these enterprises, working together is a way to make friends. A survey by General Foods International beverages and Harris Interactive found that 74 percent of employed women say they've made girlfriends through work. Women also make friends working together in community or church work. As we communicate about what needs to be done, we get to know each other and find ourselves connecting with certain individuals. As Diana Davis writes in *Fresh Ideas for Women's Ministry*, "As women pray, plan, study, and serve together, friendships develop."

But making friends by working together is not the association I want to make in this chapter. I want us to see how beneficial and enjoyable working together is, to see how it is another viable aspect of connecting and conversing. My premise is that when there is work to be done, women are better together.

Two or three are better than one

Hundreds of years ago, Ecclesiastes strived hard to achieve success, fame and riches. Along the way, he discovered those things weren't as important as he once thought. One of things he discovered in his pursuit was the power of connecting.

> *Two are better than one,*
> *because they have a good return for their work:*
> *If one falls down,*
> *his friend can help him up.*
> *But pity the man who falls*
> *and has no one to help him up!*
> *Also, if two lie down together, they will keep warm.*
> *But how can one keep warm alone?*
> *Though one may be overpowered,*
> *Two can defend themselves.*
> *A cord of three strands is not quickly broken.*
> Ecclesiastes 4:9–12 (NIV)

When Ecclesiastes wrote about the need for companionship, I doubt that he had twenty-first-century girlfriends in mind, but look at his wise words and see if they don't have applicability for today.

A good return

The first thing Ecclesiastes reminds us of is that we get "a good return" for our work when we work together. This return can be evident in a number of ways.

Increased strength. All of us have strengths and weaknesses; so, when you work alone, you bring only your strengths to the task at hand. When you engage the help of friends, you add their strengths. It could be their physical strength; some of us are stronger than others. It could be their mental strengths, it could be their talents, and it could be their influence or their energy. So many factors go into getting a job done, and what's needed will vary from job to job, but in every situation we can combine strengths to get the work done.

Increased productivity. You can get more done if you work with others. I know, I know, some of you are thinking, I can get more done alone. Certainly that is true for some kinds of jobs. If we are honest, sometimes it is an aggravation to work with others, but if we are friends working together, we often come to the job with the same kind of commitment and interest. Consequently, as we pool our resources, we get more done.

Increased enjoyment. When we have friends at our places of employment, then our attitude may improve about work and its corresponding responsibilities. We may look forward to going to work or it doesn't seem to be as much of a hassle if friends are there. Or we may find ourselves functioning better because we click with a co-worker. In talking with each other, your friend's creativity feeds yours and your passion ignites hers. This can even be good for the employer. Personnel management specialists say that when people have a best friend at work they are more likely to be "engaged" workers; they look forward to going to work and often use their hearts, minds, creativity, and passion. while working.

Increased resources. Women united around a common cause or vision can pool their resources. The Galilean women used their *"resources to help Jesus and his disciples"* (Luke 8:3). The resources we pool could be material ones such as the Galilean women had. They used their financial means to support Jesus and the Twelve. The resources could be the connections we have, who we know. It could be our talents such as decorating, calligraphy or cooking; it could be our mental juices. Around a table, in conversation, we can explore what might be and what we can do. One of the reasons I like to work with others is that they think of things that do not occur to me. They bring their expertise, their vantage point, their experiences to the dream table, and we get a good return on our mental work.

Help for getting up

Work takes physical and mental energy, not that you didn't know this! I mention it to remind you that we can get weary working. You get tired. You start counting the cost. You may want to give up. You're afraid you will never reach your goal. Too much is expected of you. You never expected it to be like this when you agreed to do the job or when you responded to God's call.

Work, particularly when it is about reaching a goal or doing missions or ministry, can become discouraging especially when results aren't forth coming. If we have someone who believes in the goal or who believes in us collaborating with us, she can be an encouragement. She can perk us up when we get down. She can ignite our hope and make it less likely that we'll cave under pressure.

The support of others can be crucial in completing a big job. Friends are aware of each other's triumphs and failures. They encourage one another, offer their own expertise, and pray.

I had barely gotten started following God's call to organize retreats for women when Bob and I moved. Everything was already in place, including my planning committee, in the state where we lived. I wanted to follow through in following God's call so I went ahead with the retreat even though I would be living in another state, 300 miles away. Alone, handling the details, I would have times of discouragement even though I kept in touch with the team members through email. How encouraged I would be, though, every time I returned to the area for a face-to-face meeting. Over coffee around a table, my doubts and anxieties faded, and my spirits lifted. My desire to follow the vision God gave me was renewed. Into a little circle of planners, of friends, encouragement replaced discouragement. Could this be part of what Ecclesiastes had in mind when he referred to warmth?

They will keep warm

Most probably Ecclesiastes was referring to physical warmth in this passage, but his words remind us there are many kinds of warmth. For example, working together can add warmth to life. It brings enjoyment, fellowship and enrichment. Working together as friends adds joy and often fun to the experience.

As mentioned above, the Galilean women used their resources to minister to Jesus and the apostles (Luke 8:3). I once queried more than 60 women, asking them what they thought those resources were. Most said cooking. What if it had been cooking instead of financial resources? What if there had only been one woman to do all the cooking day in and day out? What drudgery the job would have been even though she was cooking for her Master, someone she loved! How exhausting the work would have been! Oh, but how the atmosphere changes when several women cook together. Joy enters the camp! As the bread is kneaded, vegetables are chopped, and stew is stirred, girl talk takes place. The work no longer seems like drudgery nor is it as tiring.

Shared conversations are a part of the fellowship of work. When my oldest son got married, the wedding was on the East Coast. Most of my extended family lives in the Midwest and so many of them weren't able to attend his wedding. When Jim and Robin started planning a trip to visit us, I decided to throw a party for my extended family to introduce them to Robin. Since family members would be driving anywhere from 70 to 200 miles for the event, I wanted to serve a sit down meal. I expected around 50 people so this was going to require some work! I asked two friends to help me—Sue to help with the cooking and Barbara to help with the decorations. Now my husband was quite willing to help, so was our son Ben who lives with us, and Sue's husband and Barbara's husband were willing too, and they all helped before the party was over, but in the planning I needed some girl talk. Naturally planning the menu and the decorations called for lunch where we gals could discuss all the details and look at the party from every angle, weighing various options—something I doubt the men would have had much patience with. There was joy in the Poinsett Planning when I had friends to assist me in getting the job done.

They will not be overpowered

When Jesus went to Jerusalem for the Passover, even when it was dangerous, the Galilean women followed Him. They were present at the cross when Jesus was crucified even though it was not a place for women. Most of Jesus's male friends deserted Him because it was dangerous to be associated with a criminal, but the women were huddled there together. How much different it would have been if any one of them had to try to go it alone. Having companions who share the call or the same desire increases our courage.

Courage is often required when we are trying to effect a societal change or do missions and/or ministry. We aren't called just to the safe places of this world so having someone to respond to the call with us keeps us from being overpowered by our fears. We link arms together to face the challenges before us.

Another kind of protection we may need is protection against criticism and misinterpretation. On the job, leading a mission trip, or teaching a Bible study, we open ourselves to criticism. It goes with the territory, but friends who work with us, who know our hearts, can respond to that criticism or misinterpretation possibly dispelling damaging rumors.

Part of the wisdom in planning together is that others can protect you from making mistakes. None of us has the kind of insight where we can see all the possible ramifications from our efforts. Working with others can help us see pitfalls we never thought about.

The wisdom of Ecclesiastes helps see how beneficial working together is. It increases our effectiveness, gives us needed support, adds enjoyment to the experience, and protects us in several ways. Admittedly these things are possible for men, too, but I think women have an edge that makes them better together.

The conversational edge

When speaking at a woman's conference, the coordinator of women's ministry for the host church told me she had a team of 50 women. I was amazed! She told me how she had committees planned to cover everything—the luncheons, the Bible studies, the nursing home ministry, the funeral dinners, and more. With everything organized and committees to take care of everything she thought she could just let women's ministry take care of itself. It would function as an efficient machine, but it didn't. The women weren't satisfied. They needed to connect. To function as a ministry team, they needed to talk. Fellowship and conversation were important components to their ability to work together and to have joy in ministry.

I understand their sentiment. To me, times to meet together with other women to plan women's events are very special. I count it a privilege and a joy to percolate ideas, to consider various possibilities and to plan with a group of women around a table. In unhurried conversations, the talk becomes lively and animated. Creative juices flow. The energy level rises. Ideas sparkle. Solutions are born. I'm stimulated, energized, renewed, and encouraged by this kind of talk. I think this is why I appreciate so much the scene of the women going to the Jesus's tomb and *talking* as they went. Perhaps their conversation went something like this.

"Mary, how are we going to get into the tomb to anoint Jesus's body?"

"At this point, I'm not sure," Mary Magdalene replied as she walked briskly.

"The door is so heavy and it was sealed by the Romans, remember?"

"Yes, I remember," she said as she continued undeterred toward the tomb.

"And what about the Roman soldiers guarding the tomb?" asked Joanna. "Do you think they will let us near the tomb? Will they chase us away?"

"I hope not. Let's believe God will make a way."

"I wonder where the apostles are this morning," said Susanna. "Do you think one of them might be there to help us?"

Anyone overhearing their conversation would have asked, "Are you women crazy? What makes you think you can roll that big stone away? Even if you could, the Roman soldiers guarding the tomb are not going to let you near it."

You may have experienced something like this if you and some friends have kept insisting, *something needs to be done!* Maybe it was a change that needed to be made at your children's school, a Bible club started in your neighborhood, a vacant lot that needs to be cleaned up or someone needing to run for office. As you talk, it occurs to you, *We can do something!* And you commit yourselves to working together to get the job done. You roll up your sleeves and plunge in together even though you don't know how it will all transpire. You just know you are excited and committed, and together you will see the job through.

By acknowledging the blessings of working together, we are not saying that problems don't occur. Some experts advise against making friends at work; it does have its challenges. Hurt feelings and miscommunication occur within all kinds of groups but still I wouldn't want to miss the return, the support, the warmth, and the protection that comes from working with women. When I left home for the first retreat I planned, I said to Bob, "Even if the retreat fails, it will have been worth the effort for the experience I have had of connecting and conversing with my committee of women."

11

When I Need Two or Three

- When the Galilean women headed toward Jesus's tomb, they had no idea what would await them there. Simply intent on completing the ministry that had started, they were rewarded for their effort. They were the first to learn that the tomb was empty, that Jesus was alive!

- When Mary may have needed some confirmation that what she was experiencing really was of God, Elizabeth had reassuring words for her. In a loud voice, she said to Mary, *"You are the most blessed of all women, and blessed is the child you will bear!...How happy you are to believe that the Lord's message to you will come true!"* (Luke 1:42,45).

- When Paul arrived in Philippi, Lydia's heart was ready and receptive to the gospel because she had been meeting with a group of women for prayer (Acts 16:13–14). Because she worshiped God, she *"opened her mind to pay attention to what Paul was saying"* (Acts 16:14) and became Paul's first convert in Europe.

*W*hen believing women come together, something spiritual often transpires. It could be an unexpected blessing, a confirmation that God is working, a receiving of God's realness, or any number of other things. Spiritual things happen when two, three, or more believers gather together and talk.

Prayers are answered

The Bible promises answers for those who pray together. Jesus said, *"I tell you that if two of you on earth agree about anything you ask for, it will be done for you by my Father in heaven"* (Matthew 18:19 NIV). Obviously, we all know that we can experience answered prayer individually, but praying with others can add another powerful dimension to our prayer life.

For example, sometimes we can't seem to get a breakthrough in our private praying. I remember being in a position like this once when I needed confirmation and reassurance. I had been trying to be a spokesperson for God but had not been successful. I wondered whether I should quit being a writer and a speaker and move on to something else. I couldn't get a definitive answer from God so over lunch with Susan (whom you met in chapter 1) and Anne (not her real name), I described what I was experiencing. I said, "I really need God to show me in a clear way whether to keep writing and speaking."

When we three prayed out loud together, which is the way we usually concluded our lunches, Anne prayed for me. She asked God to reveal His answer through my husband. When she said that, I realized I should have been considering Bob's opinion. After all, my future was intertwined with his, so I agreed with Anne when it was my turn to pray and so did Susan.

That weekend in a lazy Saturday afternoon conversation, Bob brought up my writing and speaking. He said,

"I've been thinking about our future. I wish we could move somewhere where you would have access to a large library for research."

My ears perked up. I asked, "Are you saying what I think you are saying? Do you think I should continue writing and speaking?"

"You've got to. This is what God has called you to do."

Just the kind of answer I needed! It was clear! Plus it had a solidness to it because Susan, Anne, and Bob had all been involved. It could never be said that the desire to write and to speak was wishful thinking or my imagination. It was an answer that could be depended on it, and I did depend on it in the days ahead because nothing had changed. Pursuing writing and speaking was still difficult, but now I had directive that I could hold on to!

His presence is felt

One of the most exciting and meaningful things that can come out of believers gathering together is to experience Christ's presence. Jesus said, *"For where two or three come together in my name, there am I with them"* (Matthew 18:20 NIV).

The phrase *"in my name"* may sound strange to our ears, but it did not sound strange to Jesus's listeners. In His day, the expression *the name* was used in a very special way. It did not mean simply the name by which a person was addressed or called, such as Joan or Sandra. It meant the whole nature and character of the person insofar as it can be known.

To meet in Jesus's name means we come together believing that He is the way, the truth, and the life. To do this, we might verbally acknowledge His presence, but even if we don't say the words, we still can meet in His name by being attentive to others, listening to what they have to say, and being attuned to the leadership of the Holy Spirit.

In response to our meeting in Jesus's name, Jesus reveals Himself. He makes His presence known among us. Sometimes His presence is visible by the look of peace that comes over the faces of women. Sometimes a heavenly hush falls over the room and you find yourself wanting to sing "Surely the presence of the Lord is in this place"; or tears will start slipping down the cheeks of some of the women. Often it is just a powerful sense that "He is here." His presence is so real you feel as if you can reach out and touch Him.

This is not to say Jesus isn't present in times of solitude. Of course, He is, but I've found His presence is more perceptible when we encounter Him as a group than when praying alone. When we experience His presence with others who also acknowledge Him, our faith is affirmed and refreshed. We *know* He is not just a figment of our imagination; we know that the invisible God we worship is truly real.

Healing is experienced

James wrote, *"Is any one of you sick? He should call for the elders of the church to pray over him and anoint him with oil in the name of the Lord. And the prayer offered in faith will make the sick person well; the Lord will raise him up"* (James 5:14–15 NIV). His words remind us that sometimes you just can't pray through your ailments alone. In your pain or fear your faith is almost zilch. You can't bring yourself to articulate your need let alone believe that God would heal you. James' solution was to "call for the elders." In other words, *share that need with others*. For some of us, with very personal needs or with a hesitancy to share, we may need to call for strong faith-believing women to pray for us. We can lean on them to offer faith-believing prayers on our behalf.

James also implies that sin may be part of a sick person's problem. He encourages us to confess those sins to each other (James 5:16*a*)—something that may be harder to do than to ask for physical healing. But confession may be just the avenue we need to experience God's forgiveness.

As we confess, other people can be His instruments for learning God forgives us. Long ago, God granted the power to express His forgiveness to His followers. It was during one of Jesus's resurrection appearances. As Jesus showed His followers His hands and side, He said, *"Peace be with you! As the Father has sent me, I am sending you.' And with that he breathed on them and said, 'Receive the Holy Spirit. If you forgive anyone his sins, they are forgiven; if you do not forgive them, they are not forgiven'"* (John 20:21–23 NIV).

> Unexpected blessings, confirmations, reassurance, answered prayer, God's presence, healing, and forgiveness are among the spiritual possibilities.

This doesn't mean that we do the actual forgiving of another's sins, but it does mean that it is our privilege to convey God's forgiveness. If we recognize a woman is repentant, then we can assure her of God's forgiveness. This can be through words or actions. As we interact with each other, we may actually voice words of forgiveness, but God's grace may also be extended in a woman's eyes, in her facial expression, in the touch of her hand or the hug she gives on parting.

Unexpected blessings, confirmations, reassurance, answered prayer, God's presence, healing, and forgiveness are among the spiritual possibilities that may transpire when we meet with others in the name of Jesus. I say *may* because we can't predict which of these will occur, and neither can we demand that any of them occur. What we can do is prepare an environment where God can work. To prepare that environment, we need to talk.

Talks link us together

Verbalizing is the way we bring ourselves to the group; it is the way we connect with each other. If you have been meeting with a group of women for a long time, you may have forgotten how important this component is. But if you have just moved or if you are new to a group, you know that talking is how we get to know each other. We learn what each other's values are and what their needs are. We learn whether we are going to click or not. When Beth was invited by Joan and Sabrina to start meeting regularly for lunch and prayer, she thought, *This is not going to be a good fit.* Joan's house was so large and well-furnished and decorated that she couldn't help but compare it to her small house with its thread-bare carpet. Sabrina's house wasn't as well decorated, but her husband had a good job that paid well and had great medical benefits. Beth and her husband were barely scraping by. After the first meeting at Joan's luxurious home, Beth went home and told her husband, "I could never admit to having money problems with them. They would never understand." But Beth went back to the next meeting and to the next. As the three talked, she discovered they had things in common. In fact, Joan and Sabrina also had money problems, just different kinds. From then on, she felt a kinship with them and freedom to talk about her problems.

Sharing about personal needs and joys fosters love and understanding. As we talk, we feel closer to each other and, consequently, closer to God. As we join spiritual hands (through linking with each other), we form a circle that God can step into.

Talk reveals needs

Talking opens the way to healing and lets others know how needs can be met. If you are sick and in need of healing, there's a chance others might recognize your need, but often we are dealing with things others can't see. If you don't say something, if you don't "call for the elders," your friends will not know to pray or how to pray. While women are very sensitive, we are not mind-readers.

Also, your verbal admission may be your first step to healing. The admitting of a need reflects willingness for God to work and gives others a chance to assist with that healing. Sharon (not her real name), one of the survey respondents, happened to attend the last session of a Bible study being taught by her new pastor's wife, Lucy (not her real name). During the Bible study, Lucy spoke about her call to women's ministry. She said that God kept sending her women who were sexually abused.

Sharon said: "Right then I admitted out loud that I had been sexually abused. I had never told anyone other than my family and the support group that I had been attending for two years, and this announcement was in front of women whom I was going to church with. It got really quiet, and then Lucy pointed at me and said, 'OK, let's talk later.'" When they talked, Lucy agreed to help Sharon.

Lucy was already meeting with another woman who had been sexually abused when Sharon admitted she had been. The three of them started meeting as a group on a regular basis. Eventually other women joined them and they studied a book called *Helping Victims of Sexual Abuse* and worked through their past until they found healing. This healing would not have happened if Lucy hadn't said she worked with abused women and if Sharon had not revealed that she had been sexually abused. Talk made healing possible.

Talk leads to agreement

The sharing of words is important to coming to an agreement, the agreement that Jesus said was important to receiving answers to prayer (Matthew 18:19*a*). That's why when Mary Rose, my current prayer partner, and I meet, we talk to each other before we talk to God. We describe our prayer concerns to each other, and we also do some gentle probing. We ask each other questions such as, "What do you need most from God at this time?" "What exactly are we going to ask God for?" "What do you expect God to do? Do you believe He will do it?"

One day when we were trying to figure out what Mary Rose needed most from God, she thought it was possibly related to her busy schedule. She was experiencing a hunger she could not articulate. I said, "Tell me about your schedule."

Mary Rose described what she did every day, Monday through Sunday, and I took notes. When I saw it all before me on paper, I realized her life was all wrapped up in meeting the needs of people. I said, "What about your mind? When in your schedule do you take time for mental stimulation?"

Tears welled up in her eyes, and she said, "That's it! I don't have time to read, to think, and to study—and I need it." We knew then how to pray, and it was powerful praying because we were able to pray in agreement.

Perhaps these reasons for talking are why many women prefer small groups that use a "communicative mode." They desire an environment where questions are asked and sometimes answered, where input is solicited and thoughts are shared. In other words, where they can talk!

"I need friendship, Christian interaction, and Bible study."

"I love women's Bible study groups that have lots of interaction."

"I am currently in a Bible study with five other women and we share our prayer requests and daily pray for each other."

"I enjoy ladies Bible studies because I need to participate in honest discussions and receive hugs and forgiveness."

"We have Bible study/discussion, and it is also a time of encouraging one another, sharing openly (everything is kept confidential) and building each other up in the Lord. Many ladies have told me how much they need this type of meeting."

In this "circle-the-wagons" approach, gathering in Jesus's name, we can be strengthened so we can withstand the onslaught and attacks of the secular world and survive the general eroding that stress takes on our lives. As Carla said, "A long time ago, I knew I'd never make it as a Christian without being able to develop relationships held together by prayer. Praying with cherished friends throughout the years has helped me persevere in life."

I agree and that's what I needed after I moved. Long before a Mary Rose showed up, I needed a Susan or an Anne in my life to help me persevere. Just any kind of talk wasn't enough for me. I needed talk in the name of Jesus. The question before me was *Will I be able to find it?*

Part 3

The B's of Friendship

12

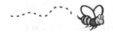

Be Friendly

*A*re you beginning to see how beneficial connecting and conversing with other women can be?

- Talking with women who understand reduces our stress and refreshes our spirit.
- Connecting and talking with other women help us successfully navigate the wanted and unwanted changes that come along in life.
- Talking and "comparing notes" also helps us understand and encourage each other as we move through the various stages of life.
- We increase our power, creativity, and joy when we work together.
- We broaden and enhance our ability to experience God when we talk in His name.

Considering all the benefits, wouldn't you say that these connections are almost crucial to our well-being?

Vital connections

Connecting with others is indeed important to our well-being. It also affects our physical health. Many studies of large populations have shown that people who describe themselves as lonely or as having little social support are more likely to die prematurely and to have infections, high blood pressure, insomnia, and cancer. Women who connect with other women throughout adulthood are happier, stronger, and even healthier individuals, yet many of us find it difficult to have vital connections.

Women's lives are complicated and tightly scheduled. Many of us have so many responsibilities that we don't have time to talk about our feelings or encourage someone else to talk. We worry about how we're going to get our work done or meet our responsibilities. Meeting deadlines and maintaining schedules doesn't allow time for sharing.

Some women's lives are so intense they don't know they are without vital connections until a crisis hits or something unexpected happens. Then they may long for someone to talk to, but there's no one to call. This happened to me several years before I moved. This is why I was so conscious about the need to make friends once I moved. I didn't want to be without friends again.

As an adjunct college instructor, my employment was always uncertain, yet it never felt that way because my classes always made. I usually taught year round, but then came the summer when not enough students enrolled. My classes didn't make, so suddenly I had time on my hands.

That same summer Bob was very busy. He was immersed in an important project, working days and evenings. Our son Ben had a fulltime, daytime summer job. When he came home from work each evening, he would shower, quickly eat dinner, and be on his way to hang out with friends. One evening as I watched Ben drive away, I thought, *I wish I had someone to hang out with*.

Wait a minute! I have friends, I reminded myself. Susan was my friend and a good talker, but she was gone a lot that summer. When she was home, she was very busy, so I hesitated to bother her. I had other women in my life, friends to talk with if I saw them in Walmart, in the post office, or at the beauty shop. But what I didn't have was someone who would be willing to put the brakes on life for a while, share some time and talk, and give back that "I-know-how-you-feel" response. Call me crazy, but what I longed for those evenings Ben spent with friends was someone to sit on the patio with me. We could watch the sun go down, marvel at the fireflies, sip lemonade, and process life together. I wanted *girl talk*, but there wasn't anyone to call.

I'm not the only woman to experience something like this because life changes and we change. You may have connections that last a lifetime. Some people do, but on the other hand you may wake up one morning and find, like I did, that you are without lunch mates.

Life's ever-changing landscape

You may finish high school as bosom buddies and swear that you will always be friends, but you choose to go to college and she enters the military. As you say good-bye, you vow you will always stay in touch, and yet as time passes, you have less and less to talk about. The conversations, when you do have them, become strained until finally you quit calling.

If you both get married around the same time, it can be great fun and kinship as you share every detail, but if one of you gets married and the other doesn't, then this choice may separate you. It may not happen at first, but eventually you find you don't have much in common anymore.

But just as marriage separates so can divorce. When a woman gets divorced, she may find that her married friends stop calling. And if she hadn't maintained connections with her single friends, she may have no one to talk with.

When a woman has a baby, she often gets caught up in the wonder and responsibility of having a child. What matters most to the new mother may not matter at all to her childless friend. The camaraderie of "we're in this together" that they enjoyed before the baby diminishes, and sometimes it is too much of a challenge to overcome.

When women's employment situations change, they may experience a change in relationships. Amy faced a loss of vital connections when she left the work force to become a fulltime mother. She wrote, "I experienced an almost complete change in friendships. Very few work friends transferred with my new life as a mother. How hard it was!"

During the earnest years when women are consumed with marrying, raising children and establishing careers, they can have such all consuming responsibilities that friendships are neglected. They may not even be conscious that it is happening until the earnestness diminishes and they have time on their hands.

Retirees often miss the people with whom they interacted with daily. Women who have spent much of their adult life in jobs outside the home may have developed a network of friends at their workplace. Over lunches, during coffee breaks, or while waiting to use the copy machine, they shared the details of their lives, laughed together, bolstered and encouraged each other. Once they retire, they may find themselves friendless.

Something else women around retirement age face is the number of their friends diminishing as they start dying. Even Dr. Joyce Brothers admits to feeling the pain of this. She wrote in *Parade* magazine (February 16, 1997), "I find that one of the hardest parts of growing older is the extent to which we are diminished by the loss of those close to us. The friends I had...for the most part, died. Their absence remains a hole in my life."

Moving also threatens relationships. In today's transient society, a woman makes a close friend and finds she has to move, or her friend has to move. "The twenties are the most mobile decade in women's lives," writes Sandy Sheehy in the book *Connecting*. "In any given year, about a third of Americans age twenty to twenty-nine change their primary residence. If a woman this age doesn't move, chances are one of her close friends will." As Robin a survey respondent, wrote, "It's hard having friends especially from college spread so far apart, all over the US. You can't just pick up the phone and plan an impromptu outing."

Robin was learning, as I think all women should, that friends don't always stay friends forever. Because conversations and connections are so vital to our well-being, we need to be aware of this so we'll be aware of what affects relationships. What we have discussed here so far has been changes that occur due to the nature of life, but there are other things that can disconnect us.

Friendship interrupted

The Apostle Paul was a man with many friends. He seldom spent time alone. Almost always someone was with him, helping him in doing God's work. The New Testament mentions nearly 90 individuals that are connected with Paul. He lived and worked with Priscilla and Aquila. He always had traveling companions even when he was a prisoner. He wrote letters to his friends Timothy, Titus, and Philemon. He has a long list of friends in Romans 16 in which He refers to three of them as "dear friends": Epaenetus (16:5), Stachys (16:9), and Persis (16:12).

Paul's relationships, though, were not without difficulty. He and his good friend, Barnabas, the one who encouraged him in his early ministry, parted ways over differences in opinion regarding young John Mark. Demas deserted him at a crucial time in Paul's life (2 Timothy 4:10) as did

Hermogenes and Phygelus (2 Timothy 1:15). His friend, Alexander, did him great harm (2 Timothy 4:15a).

People disappoint us or misunderstand us. Friends break up. Friends hurt each other. Sometimes they hurt us, and sometimes we are the ones doing the hurting. Miscommunication and hurt feelings contributed to my lonely summer.

I said I was hesitant to call Susan because she was busy, but it also had to do with the fact that she, Anne, and I *had been* a threesome. The three of us got together around every three weeks or so for lunch and coffee. We took turns meeting in each other's homes. We set a lovely table and shared our lives over salad. Then over coffee and dessert, we shared our most pressing needs—those things we wanted to pray about. As we finished our coffee, we prayed together. These times were so precious that often we ended our times together by asking, "Do you think we will still be doing this when we are in our 80s?" "Yes!" we would exclaim and high five each other. We were friends forever. But forever didn't last because I did something wrong.

The call that shouldn't have been

Someone from the church we three attended called me about some news she had heard concerning Anne. I insisted the rumor was wrong, but the caller, a woman I respected, thought otherwise. Anne and Susan were scheduled to come to my house the next day for our regularly scheduled meeting. If what this woman was telling me was true, then as a prayer partner and sister-in-the Lord I felt I needed to confront her. I mean, *How could we pray together with this awful thing standing between us?*

The news, though, was so outrageous that I couldn't see myself even saying the words out loud to Anne in face-to-face conversation. I thought, *I must know if this rumor is true before I mention it to her.* I thought perhaps her son would be up front with me about it. I didn't know where

Zack (not his real name lived) so I called a local hang-out he frequented. The owner, a close friend of Zack's, wanted to know who I was and why I wanted to talk with him. I told him my name and that I needed to talk to Zack because I was concerned about his mother. He said Zack was not there.

When I hung up, I knew immediately I had taken the wrong approach. I should have had the courage to talk with Anne, or I should have consulted with Susan first; realizing this I did nothing else. I prayed God would help me know what to do the next day at lunch.

That evening while I was preparing dinner, the doorbell rang. I went to the door, and there was Anne's father. He handed me a letter from Anne and told me she would not be at my house the next day.

I opened the letter from Anne in which she said, "Why have you been calling all over town about me?" and "I no longer want to be a part of this group."

> That evening while I was preparing dinner, the doorbell rang. I went to the door, and there was Anne's father. He handed me a letter from Anne....

I called Susan and told her what happened. She went with me to see Anne. I wanted to apologize and ask her forgiveness, but Anne would not see me.

Eventually, after some time passed, I made contact with Anne. She said she forgave me, and we hugged, but she refused to come back to the group. Today, if we ended up at the same event, I would introduce her as a friend, and she would me, but there was no undoing what I had done. There was no going back to being friends who could talk and pray together.

Susan and I tried to go on with our regular meetings, but it wasn't the same. We were like a three-legged stool with one leg missing; the loss was just too great so we stopped meeting on a regular basis. This vital connection—lunch with friends—had been snapped, and I grieved the loss tremendously. Fortunately, at the time, I was teaching. In preparing for and being in the classroom, I functioned, but then summer came and my classes didn't make. Suddenly I had time to do all those "someday-when-I-get-time" jobs, but none of them interested me. Loneliness closed in around me. I wanted and needed a friend.

Praying for a friend

As the summer wore on and my loneliness continued, I began praying for a friend.

What I had in mind was someone who would come along who would fill Anne's spot. We would click immediately, but I had a lot to learn about building relationships. Perhaps that's why God answered my prayer with a verse instead of a person.

As I persisted in asking, a Bible verse I learned as a child repeatedly entered my mind: *"A man that hath friends must shew himself friendly"* (Proverbs 18:24 KJV). At first, I was puzzled by God's answer. *Why was God answering me with a Bible verse instead of giving me the friend I wanted and needed?* On the surface, the verse seemed simple enough, so why was God continually bringing the verse to my attention? I was a friendly person. I knew how to meet and to greet and keep a conversation going. Could there be something more to being friendly? What did that mean? Did it mean more than smiling, having a firm handshake, and being quick to say hello? Could God be trying to teach me something?

Prior to this, I confess I hadn't given much thought to making friends and keeping friends. You may be the same way, especially if you have lived in the same area all your life. You have never known a time in your life when you didn't have someone to call, so you've never thought about how to connect with others. Even during earlier times of loneliness, I never considered learning *how* to make friends and to keep them. I assumed that friendships just happened. This wasn't an area of life that needed concentrated effort, but God convinced me otherwise.

Once I started studying what being friendly means, I learned many things about making and keeping friends. There wouldn't have been that slap-happy conversation with Cathy, Holly, and Debbie that I mentioned at the beginning of the book, if I hadn't come to understand what being friendly means. Neither would there have been new friends after I moved. I've learned that if I am to have vital connections, establishing them and cultivating them is something I must work at.

How about you?

Are you on your first job right out of college and feeling lonely?

Are you a new mother wishing you had someone to talk diapers and formula with?

Are you a pastor's wife surrounded by people but wishing for someone you could really talk to?

Are you a widow, adjusting to life, without your husband and needing someone who will allow you to grieve?

Are you an over-burdened career women, juggling too many balls and longing for a moment when you can let the balls fall to the floor and be yourself with someone?

Are you newly divorced and wondering, *How do I make friends as an adult?*

Are you someone who wants to cultivate relationships?

Do you want to know how you can better work with women?

Are you someone with 250 friends on Facebook and wishing you could have 275 then maybe you wouldn't feel lonely?

Are you craving conversation, community, and connection?

If you want vital connections, then I ask you to read on. In the remainder of this book, I am going to share with you what I learned about establishing and keeping lunch mates—women you can really share yourself with in face-to-face encounters. These are things every woman ought to know if she wants to have vital connections, because it is out of a pool of friendliness that we most often gain those relationships where we can call and say, "Can you meet me for lunch?"

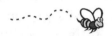

13

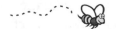

Be Available

*W*hat are the obstacles that keep women from connecting and having conversations? For many, the major obstacle is time. Everyone from high-level executives to stay-at-home moms seems to have the same complaint these days: *We don't have enough time.* This was Cathy's complaint when she started graduate school. She said to me: "I just feel so separated from everyone! All I do is work and school. I hardly remember life as I used to know it!" Life as she once knew it had time for unhurried conversations, but once she started working and doing graduate school at the same time, there was no time for girl talk!

Why finding time is hard

Whatever options they choose, women are chronically short of time. If you pursue a career, there are many demands on your time. If you choose to be a stay-at-home mom, your life is full of responsibilities. If you choose to homeschool your children, your responsibilities increase. If you combine any of these roles, as many women do, then your schedule is even more crowded.

You would think when you get older, after the children are raised, or you have hit a plateau in your work, you would have all kinds of time on your hands, but other things quickly fill it. Even many retired people talk about not having enough time. It's like once you clear a spot, something quickly fills the space.

If crowded schedules aren't problematic enough, other things clamor for our attention and often get it. For example, the BlackBerry you bought to make your life more efficient also made you more accessible. You never seem to be in a place where no one can reach you so you are always on, always alert, always thinking, always reacting.

In addition to crowded schedules and constant accessibility, we have relationships that need tending. You may be a wife with a marital relationship to cultivate. You may be a mother with children to look after. You may be a daughter needing to spend time with your parents. You may be a church member and feel like you to need to connect with other members of the congregation. You may be a boss and have employees under you, or you may be an employee with a boss to please. You may begin to feel like you just can't relate to another person. Besides, with so many people depending on you, having lunch with a friend would seem like an unaffordable luxury. Nancy Ann Jeffrey in "Whatever Happened to Friendship?" (*The Wall Street Journal*, March 3, 2000), tells about one woman who explained to her 11-year-old son that she was planning to take a rare night out with a girlfriend. She "was so apologetic that he threw his arm around her shoulder and consoled her. 'It's OK, Mom, he told her. You need a social life too.'"

And for the Christian woman, she needs to consider her relationship with God. She must find time for Him. Over and over, she's heard that every Christian ought to have a devotional life, participate in corporate worship, be active in church, develop a ministry, and go on missions trips.

Then there is also *you* to consider. You are urged to make time for yourself, take care of your health, and find time to exercise. Whew! It makes me tired just to write about all that consumes a woman's time and attention.

The pressure is so unrelenting that when you do get some time you would rather zone out rather than work on connecting with another person. You prefer to hang out around the house doing nothing or collapsing on the couch to watch a movie. You are just too tired to do anything else.

In order to succeed—or to survive!—you ignore your need for vital connections, and yet, in light of what we have learned in this book, isn't that a mistake? We were meant to be sources of strength for each other. Our conversations nurture and refresh each other, so we need unpressured space for having lunch or coffee together. We need time to talk. How do we find the time? Here's what I learned about making time for relationships where we can have face-to-face conversations.

Rearrange priorities

If you are a busy woman who wants vital connections, then you may need to do what I did, and that is move friendship to a higher place of priority. With so much to do, the importance of spending time with friends can be seen as an optional indulgence, so it gets moved to the bottom of your list or off your list altogether. Friendship is the one thing you can give up or ignore in your jam-packed life.

I'm not suggesting that having friends be moved to the top of your list, because God, your family, and your work are important and deserve priority. But what I am recommending is that you stop thinking of friends as something optional. Instead, think of them as an integral component. As one woman said, "You can't wait to live your life. If you like being around women and want to continue to have a relationship, you can't put them off."

For me, this meant loosening up. I was Miss Time Management. One of the study skills I taught college students was time management, and so I read a lot about time management. I conscientiously tried to practice what I learned and taught. I guarded my time and lived a scheduled life, which included walking for exercise. I didn't even encourage women to walk with me because I would have to check in with them and wait on them. Those minutes were too precious to give up. That's how tightly controlled my life was.

I certainly had time the summer I discovered I was lonely, but my concern was about when school started again. I was certain my classes would make in the fall. When the pace of life picked up again, would Miss Time Management have time for some leisurely conversations? I determined that I would make time. I would move having women I could talk with up on my list of what's important. I prioritized by giving mental assent for devoting time to this and relaxing my schedule.

You may need to prioritize in another way. Is there some committee that you could resign from? Could you leave your house a bit messier? Could you spend less time shopping? Could you organize your life in ways that would free up some friend time? Could you pare away an activity or a commitment in order to commit to friendship? As one ministry wife said, "I had to give up being everywhere to be somewhere with a friend."

Open your eyes to opportunities

If you are short on time and want to make friends, then be conscious of the opportunities right where you are. It is not as if you have to enter unexplored territory.

Work is where many women make most of their friends, because that's where they spend most of their waking hours. Who is available at work? Who could you get to know at the water cooler, around the copy machine, in the break room or over lunch?

Many women meet their girlfriends through their children. While participating in a Parent Teacher Organization (PTO), or watching from the sidelines at a soccer game, women use that time to notice other women they might click with. New friends might even be the friends of their children! I met Cathy and Debbie through my son Joel; they were his friends first.

But maybe your life is sparse of interactive opportunities where you can easily make friends. If you are not employed and live in a neighborhood where residents wave at each other and nothing more, you may need to put yourself in places where women connect on a regular basis. Here are some suggestions.

- Pursue hobbies and interests.
- Go to adult-education classes.
- Join community service organizations.
- Get involved in a cause.
- Go to church.

Church is an excellent place for connecting because it provides a wide pool of women of all ages with varied interests but with a common faith. But the church or any organization will not be a place for connecting if no interaction takes place so you need not only to go, but to get involved. Just going and sitting in a pew and offering only a handshake or smile will not facilitate connecting, but interaction will. Here are some ways respondents interacted and developed relationships.

"I sought out younger women at church by keeping the nursery and serving on committees."

"One of the ladies from church was chairman of the pulpit committee. We got really close during the time we served together."

"An older woman and I worked closely in women's ministry programming. We worked well together, and we became very good friends. It was a mutually rewarding relationship."

Changing churches helped me. Because God led us to help a mission congregation, Bob and I left a church with Sunday morning attendance of around 400 to help out a small congregation of less than 30. In a congregation that small, you are forced to mingle! That's where my friendship with Holly began and where my connection with Cathy and Debbie flourished. I knew Holly from school where I had been one of her instructors. She was a member of the little church, and we became friends. When Cathy moved back to live in her hometown, I invited her to church. I also invited Debbie when she returned from a short-term missionary assignment. They both joined, and we became better acquainted as we interacted in a small church environment.

Finding time once you have connected

If I've learned anything from my summer of discontent, it's that I won't just find the time for conversation, I have to make it. Setting up regularly scheduled times works well for me. This means writing it on my calendar! Together we can plan for a lunch date, an early morning breakfast, or coffee on a Saturday morning.

Mary Rose, my talk and prayer partner, and I schedule time to get together once every month. We commit ourselves to keeping these times, and we are careful about the amount of time we spend when we are together. In other words, we know when to quit talking and to get back to the things God has called us to do!

For Jan and me, scheduling a set once-a-month time doesn't work as well because of our work schedules. She's a pastor's wife and an office administrator, and I'm a full-time writer and speaker. Jan is real good, though, about sensing when we need to have lunch. When those moments occur, she emails me; we check our calendars; and we reserve a time. We also make sure we plan lunch dates for each other's birthdays and for Christmas. We also travel together often, as we are both active in the same missions organization.

Scheduling time together makes it more probable that we will get together, but this doesn't mean I never do anything spontaneous. As I was walking in my neighborhood one day, a woman whom I had met and talked with briefly, pulled out of her driveway. She rolled the window down and said, "I'm going to the bank to make a deposit. Want to ride along with me?" I did, and we had a nice 30-minute, uninterrupted chat. Even small chunks of uninterrupted conversation can be beneficial.

> If you suddenly find yourself with an hour or so free, call someone: "Want to go for ice cream?" or "I've got some stale bread. Let's take the kids to the lake and feed the ducks."

Marion was certain, though, that she couldn't find time to be with a friend, even to take a short brisk walk or go out for a cup of coffee because she had two children under three and another one on the way. One day she was lamenting to her husband that she never got to be with friends and about how babysitters were hard to find. He responded, "Well, I'm here. During the time you've been complaining, you could have been talking to a friend. I'm willing to take care of the children." Sometimes the solution can be right in front of us but we can't see it.

If you suddenly find yourself with an hour or so free, call someone: "Want to go for ice cream?" or "I've got some stale bread. Let's take the kids to the lake and feed the ducks." Now who you call may have to say no because she is not free, but she will be glad you thought of her. If she is not free, then call someone else, and maybe even another person. You'll be glad you made the effort. Sometimes we put off contacting people, waiting for everything to be just right, but little spontaneous moments here and there can keep the girlishness alive within us.

I'll admit that as I started making time available for vital connections by changing priorities, opening my eyes to opportunities, and finding time to be together, I was pretty much thinking of myself. My summer of discontent helped me recognize how much I needed lunch mates in my life. That recognition was my impetus to make changes, but there was a time factor I failed to consider. I had one more thing I needed to learn—and to change—regarding making time for friends.

Making time for her

When I thought about who I could make friends with, I started with one of Ben's friends. One of the places he often went on his nights out was to Tim and Jane's house. They were both schoolteachers, and young people flocked to their house. Ben went initially because he needed help with math; Tim was a math teacher. The general atmosphere was youth conducive, where they could talk in a nonjudgmental atmosphere.

Since Jane was a teacher and she liked my son, I figured we would have two things in common! I invited her for coffee. Turns out she was not a coffee drinker; she preferred tea so we became teacup friends. She was not a replacement of Anne; the two were not alike, but even if they were, it was too early for the same kind of intimacy I had with Anne. Cultivating vital connections takes effort and patience because it may take a while. My research shows that it takes anywhere from two to three years to form lasting friendships.

I enjoyed Jane's company, as she liked to talk about books, movies, and musicals. She also had a good sense of humor, so our times together were fun. From time to time, I would "prepare a table" for her, and have her for tea after school started. At one of those teas, she invited me to help her chaperone her middle-school students to a nearby university to see *Joseph and the Amazing Technicolor Dreamcoat.* She assured me my ticket would be taken care of as a chaperone. Bless her heart, she thought she was offering me something special—something I would like since the show was religious, musical, entertaining, and free. While I graciously recognized her offer as a gift, inside I was thinking, *Yikes!! I don't want to chaperone middle-school students.* But to her I said, "Let me think about it, and I'll get back to you."

As I mulled over this invitation, another insight about being friendly dawned on me. You can't expect someone to be there for you unless you are willing to be there for them. Having a friend doesn't mean having someone available just when you need or want someone. Friendship means arranging time for her and her needs too. Being friendly means being available, which meant loosening up my tight schedule to not only find time for friends to minister to me, but to be there for them when they needed ministry. This is not to say we always have to say yes to their needs, but it is a reminder that friendship requires reciprocity.

Having women you can connect with and talk to requires intentionality, which in turn demands that choices be made, especially choices regarding time. Are you willing to make those choices? I did—and I continue to— because I need vital connections and I want the pleasure of real relationships. I've learned the wisdom of the old proverb which begins with *"Do not forsake your friend"* (Proverbs 27:10 NIV). I even said yes to Jane's invitation and went to the musical. Would you believe the students were well-behaved, and I had a good time?

14

Be Approachable

*W*hen Bob and I joined the small church with fewer than 30 members, I interacted with women of all ages. One of the women was Holly, a student of mine who I mentioned in the last chapter. When our women's group had a tea, I agreed to read a poem. When I did, I got tickled. I got so tickled, I could not continue reading. I had to hand the poem to another person to finish. Unbeknownst to me, that malfunction opened the door for Holly and me to become friends. As her teacher, I was unapproachable for developing a friendship, but she could relate to someone who makes mistakes. Some time later, she told me, "At that moment, I knew you weren't perfect." That's when I became approachable to her.

What is being approachable?

It is being open to relationships, being sociable and accessible. It is putting out the welcome mat. It is giving off vibes that say, *I'm interested in people, and I'm interested in making friends.* Being approachable is important if you want women to draw close to you, converse with you, interact with you, and possibly become your lunch mate.

To Holly, I became approachable when she learned I made mistakes like everyone else. Now, I wasn't anywhere near perfect, as you know by now! But in a teacher-student relationship, as ours had been, I was the person with authority who set the standards. Consequently, to her, I came across as someone who was perfect. Naturally, then, she never entertained the thought that we could connect, but that night at the tea, she realized I was someone she could relate to.

Actually, there was even more working against Holly and me becoming friends than the impression that I was perfect. As our relationship developed, she told me that I intimidated people. She said that I was noted around campus for having "the look." "The look" is a strong stare that parents and teachers use to control behavior. With this look I could communicate with students on the back row who were talking and not paying attention. My eyes said, *You'd better shape up or else.*

Being intimidating—not that I intended to be—and appearing to be perfect are effective tools in the classroom but barriers to developing vital connections. What other barriers might women erect that would give the impression that they are unapproachable?

What keeps you from being approachable?

You may be throwing up barriers that you might not even be aware of, discouraging women from wanting to get to know you. Here are some possibilities.

Being smug. Are you arrogant, haughty, and possibly giving off vibes that you are superior to others? You may not feel superior; it could even be your way of covering your inferior feelings, but unfortunately the vibes set up a moat around you that people won't cross to know you better.

Being sarcastic. Are you always dropping caustic remarks at someone else's expense? Maybe you do this to get a laugh, and others do laugh, but they don't draw close. Instead, to protect themselves, they keep a safe distance.

Being perfect. Cheryl Smith writing in her book *Kindling a Kindred Spirit* tells about how hard she tried to present the image of a perfect Christian. What she didn't want others to see were the uncertainties and struggles that were part of her life. When she heard that one of her teammates became a Christian, she eagerly asked her about it. "That's right," she said smiling. Then almost apologetically she added, "I have been watching you for so long and wondering what made the difference. I wanted to come and ask you, but you seemed so different from me—so perfect. I didn't think you'd understand."

> Are you always moving straight ahead at a fast pace, neither looking to your right or left? Are you giving the appearance that you can't slow down for anything or anyone?

Always in a hurry. Are you always moving straight ahead at a fast pace, neither looking to your right or left? Are you giving the appearance that you can't slow down for anything or anyone? No one is likely to reach out her arm, stop you, and say, "Slow down, you look like someone I would like to get to know."

Always talking. Isn't it interesting that we who want to have connections so we can communicate can be discouraged by someone's talking? But we also want a listener when we connect. If someone just talks on and on, never seeing or recognizing the other person is losing interest, you know she probably will not be able to give you a "I-know-how-you-feel" response. The talker has a gift for gab but not a gift for friendships.

What you are saying. When a pastor of a church I once belonged to resigned, some women bought a farewell gift for his wife. She graciously accepted our gift, but then she shocked us. She said, "I hope your next pastor's wife won't be as lonely as I have been here." We were shocked. We had no idea she had been lonely. Both she and her husband were always talking about how busy they were. She often complained, "We never have any time to ourselves." We thought we were doing her a favor by not bothering her.

There could be other barriers besides those listed here. This list is not comprehensive, but I hope I've given enough barriers for you to see things women might do even unwittingly that keeps other women from approaching them. Not many people will make the effort to climb over the barriers we erect. How can we change that? How can women become more approachable so that others will want to connect with us?

How to be approachable

If we are doing something that erects a barrier, then the obvious solution is to change what we are doing. The only problem with this is you may not be aware of the barrier you have erected. I'll always be grateful to Holly for helping me see I intimidate people. It was painful to learn this about myself, but what a useful bit of information. I've been working on being less intimidating ever since. Old habits die hard, so it is easy to slip back into that mode when I am speaking or teaching. As long as I am a speaker and a Bible teacher, I will probably have "the look" at times, but fortunately, there are many other things I can do to be more approachable.

Be the first to say hello. Don't wait for others to move toward you; instead approach them, smile, offer your hand, and say hello. Let your warmth and your interest be your calling card, and people will be relieved you are taking the first step; they will be encouraged and respond to you.

Show interest in other persons. Being approachable isn't sharing *your* most interesting experience or story, but it is being interested in someone else. Showing interest in others is a key to making friends. You start by learning the person's name, then you ask questions and really listen to the person's answers. As the Bible says, *"Each of you should look not only to your own interests, but also to the interests of others"* (Philippians 2:4 NIV).

This applies with small groups, too. Show interest in what others have to say; don't be the expert on every subject discussed or answer every question. See yourself as one of the group and don't dominate the discussion.

Identify with others by looking for common ground as you ask questions and listen. It is easier to make friends and to keep them if you are on the same wave length or have some things in common. When you are living or working in a diverse environment or when you are an outsider, look and listen for points of identity with those around you. Use these points as a springboard for conversation and connection.

Risk being imperfect. One survey respondent wrote, "I don't think I've had a real female best friend since high school. I feel like everybody's mother instead. Just because I appear strong and in control does not mean I don't have weak moments and need a shoulder to lean on sometimes myself." I have no way of knowing what was going on in this woman's life, but I wondered if anyone knew she had weak moments. She may have feared that if she exposed her weaknesses, people would like her less. But we all have weaknesses. We all goof up. Admitting to some of our imperfections may be just the key to help others identify with us and want to know us better.

Melinda Marshall, writing in *Ladies Home Journal* (February 2003), recommends throwing your insecurities on the table. She said, "I got to know my new friend Adriane when I announced at a Girl Scout function that I was ready to set my hair on fire with regard to my son's academic difficulties. Because Adriane had a daughter with similar issues, she couldn't do enough to hook me up with people she'd found helpful."

Confessing your insecurities, weaknesses, or flaws doesn't mean you should tell all or hang your dirty laundry out for others to see. Some things are meant to be told only to a therapist or to God! But it does mean admitting to foibles and frustrations.

Show respect for everyone. Don't make others feel small or foolish. Instead, respect what others have to say, appreciate where they are coming from, value their opinions, and be sensitive to their feelings. Basically, showing respect means following Jesus's command, *"do for others what you want them to do for you"* (Matthew 7:12).

Care about people and their needs. The approachable woman doesn't ask, *Do I have women in my life who nurture and minister to me?* Rather it is, *Am I a woman who nurtures and ministers to others?* When we become women who nurture and minister, then the friends will be there. They will respond to the love we exude.

Respond to overtures. Once I remarked to Les, my older friend whom you met in chapter 1, "You have so many friends, and you are always going places. I am amazed." She said, "You know why this is? It is because after I became a widow, I accepted every invitation that came along. I had seen so many widows in the early days of their losses, when they didn't feel like going anywhere, turn down invitations when people were trying to be kind. Consequently, people stopped calling. I never felt like going either, but I went anyway. I didn't decline any invitations, and I'm so glad now that I didn't."

I tried to do the same thing the year after I moved. I accepted all invitations to lunch. I no longer do that because I've established some relationships among women who understand my work schedule. To be approachable doesn't mean you have to give up your individuality or stop being self-disciplined. What it means is developing a persona that says, *I'm open to having friends.*

When people say to me, "I know you are busy" as if they shouldn't be bothering me, I respond "I have time right *now*" or "I have time for *you*." As long as I write, speak, and have a family to care for, I will be busy, but I will also need vital connections. To have them, I need to be available for relationships; therefore, I won't say no too many times. If I did, I might stop getting invitations to lunch, and I don't want that. I know the value of connecting and talking with women.

To offer these suggestions for being more approachable is not to imply that having vital connections hinges completely on approachability, but it is saying that you increase the chances. You sow more seeds for growing friendships. When you practice these things, you open yourself to a harvest of new companions. You can count on it because that's what the proverb promises. *"A [woman] that hath friends must shew [herself] friendly"* (Proverbs 18:24 KJV). Being approachable is simply part of being friendly.

15

Be Courageous

A's I studied what being friendly means and tried to practice what I was learning, I thought, *This reminds me of high school dating.* You survey the scene, checking out who looks interesting and attractive. You move closer, trying to be places where he is. You make yourself attractive (what we called being approachable in the last chapter), and eventually you work up the nerve to talk with him. All the while, you hope he will ask you out, or you will just die! Making friends may not be quite that dramatic, but there are similarities.

Checking out the scene

When you want to make friends, you are looking for potential lunch mates. This action is so automatic that you may not be conscious that you are doing it. I didn't realize this until April came in my breakout session room at a conference. She was with the sound crew, and she gave me a machine to record my session. She told me how to use it, and as she exited, I thought, *I would like to have her for a friend.* And yet, I knew nothing about her! It was love at first sight!

Some social scientists call this "falling in friendship." Two women can feel a tug toward each other in such a way that it is sort of like falling in love. I don't know if April felt any pull toward me that day, but I do know that attraction often plays a part in the process of making friends. We don't establish a relationship with everyone we encounter.

The reason we click with some women and not others is not always apparent. She just looks like someone you would like to get to know. Or, the sound of her voice is mesmerizing. Or she has an interesting way of talking that makes you want to hear more.

We are often drawn to women who share our interests. If you have preschoolers, you may look for someone whom you can arrange play dates for your children. While the children play, you two can talk. If you are athletic, you may look for someone to go to the gym with you. If you are a schoolteacher, you may look for other teachers who share your philosophy, so you can celebrate—or commiserate!—together.

Generally, we gravitate toward persons who are similar to us, and we screen out people who are dissimilar to us. We disqualify them as potential friends. These disqualifiers vary from person to person and may include such things as physical appearance, race, age, political persuasion, religion, size, economic status, and ethnicity. We filter out potential friends without realizing it so we call them *automatic* disqualifiers.

We might disregard someone of a different ethnic background because we believe things to be true about them or we just wouldn't feel comfortable around them. We might discount our minister's wife because we think she would be too holy for us to associate with. She may discount us, too, as she's been told repeatedly in conferences for pastor's wives not to make friends with someone in the congregation! If she does, she'll end up being hurt. Young women may automatically disqualify older women as possible friends because they think of them as boring and uninteresting. Some older women may categorize young women as frivolous and undependable.

The thing about these disqualifiers is that they are automatic so you might not be aware of their influence in your trying to make friends. You might be more aware of some fears that make you hesitant to make friends. It is these fears that made me associate finding lunch mates with high school dating. It is teenage angst all over again!

Fighting your fears

The thing about relationships is you long to connect with someone, and yet you fear it at the same time. What are some of the things we fear?

You are afraid if you move toward someone, someone you are attracted to, and begin to make overtures, that she will reject you. You will feel foolish, or the rejection will confirm what you've suspected, that something is dreadfully wrong with you. I wish I could tell you that rejection won't happen, but sometimes our quest for a friend does not pan out. We do not have guarantees in developing friendships. We can like someone and want to be her friend, but we may be in her disregard category!

On the other hand, even if you feel certain she would respond positively, you still may be fearful. You may be afraid that you don't have the social skills to keep the relationship going. Face-to-face relationships require thinking, sizing up a situation, quick reactions, and knowing what to say and not to say. We may not have the confidence that we can do this. Our electronic age has contributed to this. When we have friendships on the Internet, we have control. We don't have to worry about how we look, about whether we will be automatically disqualified. We can control what is said; we don't have to come up with something immediately. We can wait to answer. We can press the delete button, erase what we have written and rewrite the message. The virtual scene is always perfect. We can manage and control the relationship with very few repercussions unless we hit the "send" button too quickly! As we spend more and more time in front of a screen, our relationship muscles are atrophying so we may not have the confidence to leave a controlled environment to move to one where we don't have control.

If we were to reach out and make friends, we may be afraid we can't trust them with our conversations. This is a fear I have. When we start having lunch or coffee together and talking—when we start wanting to claim those benefits that come with chicks clicking—I'm afraid she will tell what she hears. Many of the things we discuss over lunch does not demand secrecy, and yet as the relationship develops and you want to share more, then you expect a friend to be able to judge what is OK to retell and what isn't. I'm also afraid in the retelling that she will add her own interpretation or revision of what was said. Sharing increases our vulnerability.

Not only do we want what we say kept secret, we want to be able to say it without being criticized or condemned. When we get to know another person, we want to accept her as she is and we want to be accepted as we are. We don't want lunch mates whose intent is to make us over.

"I want someone I can confide in, someone who will not be judgmental."

"I need a listener whom I don't feel I have to impress, someone whom I feel safe with, that I can admit my mistakes and insecurities to without being judged."

"I would love to have someone to listen without condemning, giving advice or trying to 'fix' anything."

"I need someone who won't judge, who will listen and give me godly advice when I need it, and will just support me no matter what I do."

"I need a listening ear who will not make judgments but will pray with and for me."

If you have been hurt by a judgmental attitude in a previous relationship, then you may be afraid to make new friends. Instead, you may want to seal yourself off to protect yourself from being criticized and judged. You vow you will never be vulnerable again. As one survey respondent wrote, "Because of hurts and disappointments in the past, I tend to shy away from close relationships with other women. I put up a wall when I feel myself getting too close to someone."

Sometimes we lose friends through death or their moving away. These kinds of losses hurt terribly, too, and you may decide you never want to be close to another person again. It's just not worth it.

If we succumb to these fears and let them stop us from reaching out, we are cutting ourselves off from experiencing the benefits of connecting and conversing. Is that what you want? This is a good question to ask because wanting friends, really wanting them, will help you overcome your fears. There are solutions to our fears, but for some the fear may be too great to overcome. With so many uncertainties, some women just aren't willing to make connections, choosing to remain lonely and longing for someone to reach out to them, but if you really want friends, you can overcome your fears.

Being friendly means overcoming

When we want friends and yet are fearful, we can go to God upon whom we can cast all our cares (1 Peter 5:7) and *"who comforts us in all our troubles"* (2 Corinthians 1:4 NIV).

We can tell Him our fears and ask Him for guidance and courage in making friends. He may respond by giving you a friend, sending someone right to you. He may open your eyes to possibilities of a woman you hadn't thought about before as being a possible friend. He may change your automatic disqualifiers. He may answer you as He did me by giving you a Bible verse, and if He does, the verse will be insightful or empowering to your situation. God will answer you in some way that is just right for you and your circumstances.

As you pray, seeking God's help in making friends, you can confess your fears to Him, and those fears will lose some of their power. At the same time, as you are verbalizing to Him, you will be acknowledging the fears to yourself. Acknowledgment gives us insight. *This is the way I am* or *this is why I'm reluctant to make friends.* This will allow us to analyze our feelings and explore solutions.

If past hurts are keeping you from making friends and having lunch mates, you may need to ask God to help you forgive those who hurt you. The way I see it is when we are Christians, we forgive friends who let us down and hurt us. This is not easy, but it keeps us from getting stuck in an unhappy, lonely place. Instead, we move on continually trying to make and to keep connections because we recognize how vital they are.

When I lost Anne as a lunch mate, it was very painful. I felt like my insides had become red and inflamed as I grieved over this loss. Since then I've lost three other close friends. These losses were not my fault. At least, I don't think they were! I didn't knowingly do something wrong as I did with Anne, but still the losses were painful. But what if I had decided, *That's it. I'm not going to make any more friends?* If I did, I would cut myself off from pleasure, support, encouragement, and life enrichment. Instead I prefer to *"count it all joy"* (James 1:2 KJV).

Fight fear with joy

As I look back at mine and Anne's relationship, I remember the wonderful experiences we had together. I wouldn't trade those experiences for anything. I'm glad we had those marvelous conversation-prayer-lunches together. Although my relationship with the other three lost friends wasn't of the same nature as with Anne, I feel the same way. I learned and grew through these connections. A part of who I am is because I spent time with these women.

Roz, a survey respondent, had a similar reaction to a relationship she lost. She had a wonderful connection with a woman who brought out the best in her, even a part of her that she hadn't even known was there. She wrote, "The Lord used her so vitally in my social development, and her radiant personality enlivened my dormant, unbeknownst-to-me sense of humor." When Roz's friend married, her life changed dramatically, and the friendship did not endure. Roz was so distraught that she became depressed. In trying to find help, she went to a church that was alive with the gospel and hope. She became a member and very involved in women's ministry. She added, "Although I'll admit losing her was a deep wound, I can't help but praise God for all aspects of my relationship with her. He brought us together; we complimented each other. He separated us in order to supply each of our needs; she got a vibrant new husband, and I got closer to the Lord."

We will be better equipped to count it all joy if we keep in mind the nature of friendship. It is voluntary. No laws are written or vows are stated that hold friends together, and the truth is some friendships weren't meant to last. Some friendships or groups will only be for a season; we connect at a particular time in our lives. The relationship serves us well but was never meant to be forever. So if a friendship ends, it doesn't mean something was wrong with us. It is simply the nature of friendship.

Even when we acknowledge our fears, seek God's help to overcome them and count it all joy, we're still going to have to do one more thing if we want vital connections. Eventually, we're going to have to ask her out! Taking action is a great antidote to fear. Doing the very thing you are most afraid of may be what you need to do to fight your fears.

Fighting fear with action

After you have checked out the scene and noticed someone you might want to connect with, it is time to move in closer for some small talk. When April came back in to my room to collect the recording machine, I asked her, "Where do you live?"

It turned out that she lived in the same county that I did. Next question: "Where do you go to church?'

She said, "We're looking for a place closer to home."

Naturally, I said, "I'd like to invite you to my church."

She said, "What kind of church do you go to"

I told her and well, you get the picture. . .

I followed up with a phone call the next week, and she came to our church—the same little church Cathy, Debbie, Holly, and I attended. Naturally, Bob and I invited her and her husband to lunch, and our friendship was launched.

If you get good feedback from your small talk, then you might want to proceed with some kind of low-risk overture toward connecting.

- "I have two tickets to a concert, would you like to go?"
- "May I sit beside you during worship?"
- "Would you like to ride along with me to the state women's conference?"
- "Our church is offering a women's Bible study. Would you like to attend?"

- "We're offering a support group for women struggling with anxiety. Would this be something you are interested in?"
- "How about taking our daughters together to the mother and daughter tea?"

In the conversations you have as you do these things together, it will further confirm whether this might possibly turn into a lunch mate relationship. Eventually, though, specific action must be taken if you are going to have unhurried, face-to-face conversations together. You will need to ask *her* to lunch. *Yikes, what if she doesn't want to go! What if I am rejected? What if it doesn't go well? What if she says no?*

There's no getting around it; there is always some risk involved in relationships. We have no way of knowing ahead of time if a person will say yes. We can be fairly certain judging by her behavior, but we never know what is really going on in a person's head or life. Sometimes you have to take chances for your health's sake. It was this kind of reasoning that helped me deal with my fear of being talked about.

In addressing my fear of being afraid others would tell what I said, I decided this was a chance I had to take. I need to talk for my mental and spiritual health, so sometimes I have to ask myself, *Is the venting (telling) of what I'm feeling more beneficial and important to me than what others think?* If it is, then I go ahead and tell a friend what's on my mind. If it isn't, then perhaps I need to keep it to myself or tell Jesus.

While we have emphasized the value of talking in this book, this doesn't mean we have to tell everything. In fact, we shouldn't. Our friends aren't to be dumping grounds, and we need to develop an inner strength to handle some things ourselves. When there is no one who understands, no one we can trust with a particular item, then we can talk to Jesus. In prayer, we can pour out our hurtful emotions to Him and experience relief and renewed strength.

Developing relationships, where you have an opportunity to talk and to listen, is an art, not a science. Results are not guaranteed, and we do a lot by trial and error. Remember it is a lot like dating, and you don't marry everyone you date. Establishing vital connections entails confronting our fears and being willing to deal with the challenges of the relationships.

16

Be Gracious

*B*eing friendly doesn't end with an invitation to lunch. Certain dynamics are needed to make the most of your time together and to sustain the connection, keeping it vital. These dynamics could be summarized by Paul's words to the Christians in Ephesus: *"Be ye kind one to another, tender-hearted, forgiving one another, even as God for Christ's sake hath forgiven you"* (Ephesians 4:32 KJV).

The Greek word for *kind* (*chrestos*) means that a person cares as much for her neighbor's feelings as she does her own. It is being adaptable to meet the needs of others. Nowhere should kindness be more evident than in our conversations.

Being kind in conversation

The hallmark of lunch mate companionship is conversation. It is the way we find out what other people like, think, and need. We converse to get to know each other, relate to each other, offer understanding, and develop trust, so both people need to share. When one person monopolizes the conversation, it stifles this process.

What the monopolizer indicates by her thoughtless behavior is that the conversation is all about me. What I think, what I know, what I feel, and what I need is what's important.

To dominate a conversation is inconsiderate and unkind. In small groups, a talkative woman can get so caught up in sharing an experience or describing a need that time runs out and others don't have a chance to share. Or her words can be so strong and intimidating that shy women refrain from saying anything. Understanding and connecting with each other is hindered.

To be sure, there will be times when one woman will do most of the talking such as when she needs to vent or talk something out, and lunch mates understand this. But if one person habitually dominates time after time, the listener or listeners will feel like they are being taken advantage of.

The better approach is to be kind by being considerate of the other person and by taking turns talking. A gracious conversationalist respects the other person and values her words. She wants to know her lunch mate's feelings, thoughts, views, and ideas. She focuses on the other person and not herself.

Taking turns speaking is practicing good manners, but the greater concern is the quality of your relationship and its sustainability. Unless all have opportunities to share, the benefits we've explored in this book will not be possible. In vital connections, there needs to be an even exchange.

Keeping it equal

For a lunch mate relationship to thrive—and survive—it is important that the relationship not get lopsided. Sometimes when we say we want a lunch mate, we really mean someone who is going to meet *our* needs, and this puts a burden on the other person. In his book *Soulcraft*, author Douglas D. Webster says what we are really seeking is a servant. He wrote, "Often when people are wishing for friends they are actually looking for servants who will meet their emotional and relational needs...seeking servants instead of friends reaps relationships full of burdens, obligations, even impositions."

While Webster calls it seeking a servant, I call it seeking a therapist. I've often had relationships where this kind of expectation exists, where I do the bulk of the listening. In fact, one woman who often invited me to lunch, said, "Why should I see a therapist at $90 an hour when I can talk to Brenda?" While we had a relationship, it was never a lunch mate relationship as has been defined in this book. She was a lonely woman, and I felt sorry for her, but after that comment I greatly curtailed my time with her because she was using me.

I think one of the survey respondents had some similar relationships. She wrote, "It seems I have always been the nurturer. When on occasion a friend unexpectedly expresses real care either in word or deed, I am deeply touched. It has been many years since experiencing an even exchange."

An even exchange is what we need in a vital connection if we are going to experience the power of conversation. All involved need to practice self-restraint, knowing when to not saying anything, but also knowing it is important to talk. A gracious lunch mate is not someone who never talks. That, too, would be detrimental to the relationship. People must be willing and able to reveal feelings, even confessing frustrations and weaknesses, to develop closeness and mutual understanding. If you don't share, the listener will feel like she doesn't know you, and you will remain lonely and unfulfilled because you aren't being your true self.

Show acceptance

The purpose of our conversations is not to change the other person, so when listening to her, we should refrain from being critical or judgmental. We shouldn't be quick to blurt out advice, and yet it can be tempting to do so. It is not necessary to live a long life or to have sage experience before we have wisdom that we would like to share. When a friend describes a problem or tells of something questionable she did, we may even feel like it is our Christian duty to correct her or to give her advice.

If her actions were outrageous, stupid, crazy, or thoughtless, we may express our judgment by a frown or a gasp. If she notices, this may cause her to freeze and to stop talking. Or it might put her in a defensive mode where words and tone escalate as she reacts to our assumed position of authority. Either way she fails to get what she really needs, and that is an "I-understand-I-know-how-you-feel" response. This is the response that ministers and nurtures.

When another woman shares her problems or hurts with us, it's natural to want to share our wisdom. The answer to her dilemma, while eluding her, may be immediately clear to us so we want to cut to the chase and start issuing advice. What she needs is to externalize her problem and feelings. One of the survey respondents wrote, "I need to be able to express my concerns, heartaches, faults, and failures without receiving Sunday school answers." In other words, "don't apply cliché answers (even if they are based on truth) to my pain without hearing me out and struggling along with me. Have regard for me."

A gracious friend will be quick to listen and slow to speak (James 1:19), showing the speaker that she has a right to her feelings and that you accept her as she is. This doesn't mean we should never give advice; it means we need to wait until the moment is right or until a woman asks us for it.

What a woman most often needs—as we have stressed repeatedly in this book—is not a "how to" or a "you ought to" or a "you shouldn't," but rather an "I-know-how-you-feel" response. This response is what will encourage and strengthen her. To be sure, there are exceptions such as in mentoring or in discipling, but most of the time it is better to be slow to advise. It is better to be a good listener.

Listen well

So important to maintaining vital connections and getting the most benefit from them is the ability to listen well. I think you will agree if you have ever had something like this happen to you.

- You start to tell something that happened to you—something you have just been dying to tell—and before you can finish your story, you friend interrupts with, "That's nothing, let me tell you what happened to me!"
- You receive some distressing news that you feel you just can't handle alone. When your committee chairperson asks for prayer requests at the end of your planning meeting, you share your news. Your voice cracks but you manage to hold back the tears. When she closes in prayer, though, the chairperson barely mentions your request. Instead, she prays around the world and back again as if she never heard the fear in your voice.
- You have never been in the hospital before so when the doctor said you needed surgery, you were alarmed and scared. When you try to tell a couple of women about it as you travel to a retreat together, they quickly launch into accounts of their own first hospital experiences, complete with humorous details. Their hilarity grates against your fear.
- You're exploring a new sales concept you have for work with a girl friend. You're glad for the opportunity because you need a sounding board

to bounce it off before you take it to the committee. When you look up from your notes, you
notice she is checking her text messages. You
can't believe it. You don't know whether to be
annoyed or hurt.

A gracious listener doesn't respond in these ways. Instead
she works at listening.

She looks at you, giving you her undivided attention. She
asks questions that show she is fully attentive and that
she has an interest in what you are saying. Her questions
encourage you to talk more. They give you the opportunity to clarify what you are saying and to add additional
information.

A gracious listener may occasionally interrupt when
something needs to be clarified, but she doesn't repeatedly
interrupt. She gives you a chance to express your thoughts
fully. She doesn't keep trying to direct the conversation back
to herself. *Instead, she does the kind thing; she* concentrates
on what you are saying.

Someone who listens well voices empathetic responses,
gives facial feedback, and seeks to understand the feelings
behind the spoken words. Sometimes she rephrases what
she hears to make sure she understands correctly. With
these actions, she is saying, "I value you and what you have
to say." One survey respondent described it as exuding
"a spirit of caring." I call it being kind and tenderhearted,
which is so important to developing the trust necessary in a
vital connection.

Building trust

What we are building through talking, accepting, and
listening is trust that we want and need in vital
connections.

"I need someone to confide in that won't tell anyone what I said because I don't want anyone else judging me on what she might tell them."

"When I share part of my soul, I need confidentiality."

"I always enjoy a good Bible study with a group of ladies, but most of all I simply seek a friend and prayer partner that can keep things confidential."

"There are aspects of my life that I have seldom revealed except to those in whom I place great confidence...it is a beautiful thing to fully trust another."

Trust usually doesn't emerge full-blown or instantaneously. As women begin to reveal themselves to each other, sharing confidences and feelings, opening up a little here and there, they gradually relax their vigilance over what they reveal to each other. This leads to closeness and mutual understanding but confidences not honored can lead to the end of a relationship.

To be lunch mates requires honesty, which means being vulnerable at times, so for a relationship to solidify and to endure, this vulnerability needs to be treated with respect and honor. A gracious listener will recognize when someone is telling something that is to be kept confidential. Now the talker may assist her by prefacing what she ways with, "I need you to keep this confidential" or "I would appreciate it if you wouldn't tell anyone this." But she may fail to assist her because she's too distraught or because it doesn't occur to her in the emotion of the moment. A sensitive, mature woman will know, though, what is all right to tell others and what isn't. A gracious woman will not tell what she hears if it would be hurtful or harmful, not even sharing it as a prayer request. A woman who hath friends keeps secrets. It is the kind thing to do.

Show affection

Important to launching a vital connection, enjoying it, and keeping it going is for the individuals to like each other, and this needs to be evident.

- The way you smile at her.
- The way your eyes light up when you see her.
- The interest you show in her life.
- The kindnesses you show her.
- The encouraging words you express.
- The compliments you offer her.
- The affirmations or support you offer.
- The staying-in-touch emails and text messages you send.
- The thoughtful things you do.

Liking each other adds to the joy of the relationship. It adds pleasure to the times of getting together. It contributes warmth and softness to the relationship. It motivates you to stay tuned to each other in between lunches. It helps maintain the commitment. It makes the "work" of being kind easier when we like someone. You are more likely to listen to someone and not be judgmental when you like her. That's why Paul encouraged us to have a tender heart. It helps us be kind, and it also helps us to forgive.

Cut her some slack

Even in the best of relationships, we will have some rough spots.

We have expectations about friendships, and we expect our friend to live up to them. When she doesn't, naturally we are disappointed. We may feel as if we have been done an injustice. It doesn't matter if she never knew our expectations, she should have!

Plus we all have some kind of idiosyncrasies. That's what contributes to our uniqueness as individuals. The more time we spend with friends, though, the more our idiosyncrasies may get on each other's nerves.

We all make blunders. That, too, is a part of our nature. We may make some wrong remarks or blurt out something totally insensitive to the matters at hand. Or even though we know the importance of keeping secrets, we may forget and tell something we shouldn't. It happens.

We all have experiences where our friends just don't get it when we try to tell them something that is really important to us. There's a gap in our understanding, and we can't seem to bridge it.

How are we going to react to these kinds of things? We might brood about our disappointments; even hold her actions against her. Never mind that she didn't know what our expectations were. She should just know! We might get exasperated by her idiosyncrasies. What's the matter with her? We could keep a tally of all her blunders, hurtful remarks, and insensitive comments. How could she say such things? We'll never trust her again with anything important.

> A woman with a tender heart will lower her expectations, forgive, and overlook. She will have a soft heart and not a record-keeping heart.

We could respond to relationship friction in these ways or we could be gracious. We can cut her some slack or as the apostle Paul put it, we could be tender-hearted and forgiving (Ephesians 4:32).

A woman with a tender heart will lower her expectations, forgive, and overlook.

She will have a soft heart and not a record-keeping heart. She will let small matters go by instead of keeping a tally. She's not into keeping score.

She will accept her friend's weird ways as that is just the way she is. Or she will give them a positive twist such as

"She's always late to lunch but I've found she's worth the wait."

She will seek clarification of ill chosen comments that disturb her by asking questions such as "What are you saying?" or "Please tell me what you meant by that?" If that doesn't resolve the situation, she will choose to let it go. She won't negate the relationship by refusing to return to the lunch table.

Something else to consider here is that we may be the ones contributing to the rough spots. It is so tempting to think only of "how she hurt *me*," but we all make mistakes. We may be the ones that are irritating. Have you never interrupted? Have you never said the wrong thing? I'm guilty, and thank God, I've had friends who have been gracious enough to overlook my remarks.

A gracious woman will apologize when she's been offensive or hurtful. She does it because it is the right thing to do and because it is like a balm applied to the rough spots of a relationship. It keeps it smooth and functioning well.

For most of us, vital connections don't just happen. They require intentionality; therefore, *"we must always aim at those things that bring peace and that help strengthen one another"* (Romans 14:19). What a challenge this is to those who possess verbal proficiency and wisdom (that includes most women)! We need help, and we have that help in Jesus Christ (Ephesians 4:32). Because God was kind, tender-hearted, and forgiving as He gave us His Son when we didn't deserve it, we can be kind, tender-hearted, and forgiving. When we do, we'll be blessed by having connections that are vital, satisfying, and lasting.

17

Be Influential

*E*arlier, before Bob and I joined the small church, Marge, an older, senior adult, invited me to lunch. She wanted me to help reach the younger women in our church. The missions organization she led was mostly older women, and it was dying. I sympathized with her, but I didn't agree to help her. I was too busy (there's that time problem again!). But I also didn't think younger women would respond to any overtures I would make. I was not a woman of influence. Since learning about being friendly, I've discovered I can be a positive influence and so can you.

Doing what comes naturally

Influencing another has not been the intent of connecting and conversing as I have written about in this book. I've promoted vital connections for life enrichment, to relieve stress, to handle change, to navigate life transitions, to get work done, and to experience God. The intent was never "Let's have lunch together so I can influence you." Nevertheless, influence may be a by-product of our interaction. It happens naturally. As we interact, we rub off on each other. As we talk, we learn from each other. As we share, we are encouraged, and as we confess, we gain insight. As we celebrate, we are inspired.

As mentioned in chapter 15, we tend to think that the best prospects for connecting are with women our age, whose marital status is the same as ours, who have children if we have children, who share similar values and interests, and who share our faith. Those kinds of connections are enriching and satisfying, but you may pass over potential friends by insisting that all your connections be with women just like you.

- What if Ruth and Naomi had insisted on being friends only with women who were just like them? Ruth was a Moabite, and Naomi was an Israelite. Ruth and Naomi were of different cultures. They were different ages. What if they had rejected the possibility of companionship?
- What if Elizabeth and Mary had declined to share together because there was a wide age difference and they lived in different provinces?

Our lives are enriched when we relate to women who are different from us. Women not exactly like us may bring a refreshing perspective on life and a wealth of experience that is lacking in just-like-me relationships plus enable us to be influential.

When she is not my age

The Apostle Paul recognized the need for women influencing women when writing to Titus, a pastor.

Teach the older women to be reverent in the way they live, not to be slanderers or addicted to much wine, but to teach what is good. Then they can train the younger women to love their husbands and children, to be self-controlled and pure, to be busy at home, to be kind, and to be subject to their husbands, so that no one will malign the word of God (Titus 2:3–5 NIV).

If you are an older woman—and we are all older than someone—you have wisdom to share. This influence is something the survey respondents indicated they wanted and needed.

"I need to have that nurturing, teaching, wisdom, comfort and reassurance from someone who has dealt with the issues of life."

"It helps to have an older woman in my life to let me know that other women have experienced what I am going through. It reassures me that all will work out in the end."

"It's nice to have someone you can share feelings and struggles with and know they have been there too. Knowing they have been there and then are where they are now encourages me that I will survive."

"I need mentoring for being a godly wife from someone who is nurturing and has wisdom."

Our lives are enriched by talking with women who are *"Older women are able to see the bigger picture and help me not to get hung up with the small stuff. They offer guidance, serve as mentors and ask good questions. Sometimes they just reassure me that I am normal and this is how life is!"*

What women want and need from an older woman is her advice, guidance, her counseling, her mothering, and her friendship. In other words, they want *talk, listening,* and *understanding*—the very things that we have seen as being important to women.

For some, the older woman was only slightly older. For others, it was years and even decades. What made her the older woman was experience. She had a proven track record for handling life, which she could share with younger women.

The name survey respondents had for the older woman varied. Many referred to her as a mentor or teacher. Others referred to her as a role model or a discipler. Some called her mother, and others cherished the wisdom of their grand-mothers. One even sang the praises of her mother-in-law! Of those titles—mentor, discipler, teacher, friend, mother, mother-in-law, grandmother, role model—the one that suits me best is friend.

Don't call me mentor

After we moved, Cathy and Debbie came to visit. Naturally, we had lots of girl talk, which must have prompted Cathy to do some thinking. After she got home, Cathy wrote me a letter. She said she wanted to change and grow in a number of areas. She listed those areas in her letter, and she asked me, "Would you be my mentor?" I was honored she asked, but after prayerful consideration, I turned her down. I preferred to be Cathy's friend rather than her mentor.

I knew once I put on the mentor garment, I would lose the ability to give her that "I-know-how-you-feel" response. Once we started working on her goals, I would start evaluating her progress. If I made suggestions, then I would expect her to follow through. "The look" would return! I might become critical and even judgmental, and I didn't want that kind of relationship with her. She was relieved by my answer as she, too, after thinking about it, sensed there would be a difference in our relationship.

This doesn't mean I don't firmly believe in the importance of being a Titus 2 woman, and that I don't applaud other women for becoming mentors. I do. I believe there is great wisdom in what Paul said, but I follow his instructions best as a woman's friend rather than as her mentor or discipler. Being a friend doesn't seem as formal or as pressured. I am freer to be myself and am not as critical. I can be her encourager, I can be her listener, I can be on her side, I can say to her: "I understand. I know how you feel."

Other older women welcome being a mentor, discipler, or teacher of younger women. Some feel specifically called to take on these roles just as God has called me to be a writer and a speaker. There's certainly a need for their ministries. In working with women, I continually hear the same kind of needs expressed as were expressed by the women in my survey. Young women want a relationship, one they can benefit and learn from, with older women.

The older woman has a wellspring of wisdom, and she can be a woman of influence by sharing it (Proverbs 18:4) if she has someone to receive it. Whether she prefers the title of teacher, mentor, discipler or friend, she can't share her wisdom unless there is someone willing to receive it. Here's where being friendly helps by bringing old and young women together. Finding time, being approachable, facing fears, taking action, and being gracious are all important to developing relationships that reach across that invisible but yet very real dividing line that separates generations. Being friendly gives women who are different the opportunity to influence each other.

Winning women

In preparing to speak to a women's ministry group on outreach, I consulted a women's ministry manual. In reading the chapter on promotion, I was stunned because not one word was mentioned about issuing personal invitations and developing relationships. It talked about brochures, news releases, newsletters, and posters. It talked about design and layout of these items and where to place them—even in bathrooms!—but nothing was said about being personable and connecting.

How odd I thought since we live in an age when flyers, posters, and newsletters are more and more being ignored as people are barraged with information. With so many groups wanting to sell us something or get us involved, we turn off the messages. We stop responding. What women need and want is someone to take a personal interest in us, to look at us, engage us in conversation, learn our name, and get to know us. Here's where being friendly assists in winning women.

Finding time. One of the first things I learned in my study of being friendly was that it takes time, and I see this time issue as so important in winning women to Christ. We need to find time to cultivate relationships where we can witness through words and actions.

Being approachable. Being warm, open, and interested in others can help us be winsome as the early Christians were. In Jerusalem, where the early church was launched, people were drawn to them. If women are drawn to us, we can draw them to Christ.

Taking action. A friendly invitation that works well in getting women to attend church, Bible studies, or women's events is "Come, go with me." This invitation says, "I'm interested in you and want to be with you." It also says, "You will not have to enter the church alone," something reassuring to many unchurched women. It just makes entering a new situation so much easier if you have someone to go with you.

Being gracious. Once newcomers are in our midst, we need to do what we can to make them feel welcome. I was recently disappointed in a group I'm program leader for. When a new woman came in, I saw her coming and motioned for her to sit at the table in front of me. As others arrived, they sat at another table. When more women came, they sat at the table where several women were sitting rather than at the table with the newcomer. Eventually this table was all bunched up with people, and they even pulled other chairs up to the table! Meanwhile the newcomer sat alone, and I tried to keep a running conversation going with her while I took care of meeting details. Fortunately, as it was time to start, our pastor's wife came in, spotted the newcomer, sat with her, and welcomed her.

Teaching women

When I was the teacher of a woman's Sunday School class, I used the power of conversation to stay in touch, to develop closeness among the members, and to unify us as a group. I lived 15 miles from the town where the church was located, and I had small children so it was almost impossible for me to have frequent face-to-face conversations with the members. Some of them, though, found their way to my house when they needed to talk. My country home provided a peaceful retreat for sharing. Over coffee, sitting at my breakfast table, looking out at the trees, problems were shared and tears were shed.

I tried to keep in touch by telephone, especially with absentees. Although we women were in the same age group, we were not all at the same stage in life. While my children were young, some of the members had older teens. When I called women on our roll who hadn't attended in awhile, I always tried to give the feel of "checking in" rather than a "why haven't you been here" approach.

When Karen had not been there for several Sundays, I called her. She was a stylish, successful career woman, and I was a stay-at-home mom. We had little in common, and yet I wanted to connect with her. After "How are you?" and "What do you think of the weather?" I faltered for something to say. As my mental wheels turned, I remembered that her youngest son was graduating from high school. I asked her about it, and to my surprise, she started crying. I listened and I sympathized with her. I could do this because I already knew I would feel the same way when my sons eventually left home! I hadn't expected someone so involved in her career to grieve over the nest emptying. I was simply trying to show interest in her life, and that interest brought her back to Sunday School. She was back in class the very next Sunday.

When *she* needs to grow

Sometimes in our interactions and conversations with other women, we notice women who need to grow. If you remember from chapter 11, Sharon admitted in a Bible study that she needed healing from sexual abuse. Lucy, her pastor's wife and the leader of the study, offered to help her. Talk was very important to that process.

Lucy helped Sharon see that her past was destroying her life. Sharon said, "I had many issues to overcome. Anger/rage was first and foremost. I had to report to Lucy every time I really raged. Over and over I would call her, and we would talk it through."

In listening, Lucy urged Sharon to go beyond the abuse—something not touched on in her support group. Sharon said, "Lucy would ask me if I was in the Word reading, studying, and seeking God for healing. She taught me about prayer and the study of God's Word. She didn't judge me, but she taught me how to handle life God's way."

Sharon said, "She was not sweet and nice to me all the time, but I would have rebelled big time if she hadn't boxed my ears once in a while. She would say, 'Sharon, I don't care whether you like me or not at this point. I care that you become the woman God wants you to be.'"

When the world needs changing

Some problems are just so huge and have been with us so long, that we tend to think that there is nothing we can do, but here again being friendly can help.

Sue wanted to do something about racial relations, a big problem in her community. She was not a community activist or a public speaker, but she wanted to do something, so she initiated a relationship with Dorothy who was of a different color and of a different economic level. Sue saw it as her little effort to change the world, and she used being friendly skills to do it. She initiated the relationship and kept it going for years.

The two women became friends, and as friends do, they laughed and talked together. They sat on a park bench in the hot summer and enjoyed cold root beer together. They talked about their children, their past, and their challenges. The pair found they had much in common, especially loving to cook for their families. Many of their conversations were about recipes, although Sue said, "There wasn't much we didn't talk about."

Over time, Sue changed. Yes, that's right, I said Sue. She was going to make everything better for Dorothy and effect change in her little part of the world, but what happened is that she became a better person. Sue said, "When someone of a different race and social class becomes your friend, it changes everything."

> With relationships that cross culturally imposed lines, whether in our community, our nation, or around the world, we can expand our influence.

With relationships that cross culturally imposed lines, whether in our community, our nation, or around the world, we can expand our influence. With international students and workers living in our community, with immigrants who have moved in to work in our areas, with various ethnic groups, and when we are on missions trips, we can have a part in changing the world simply by being friendly.

Being friendly is not complicated; the concepts expressed in the last few chapters are simple enough to understand, even simple to put into practice if we are willing. Perhaps that's why the message of this book is needed; it reminds us of what is possible and encourages us to be willing. In our disconnected, I-don't-need-anyone-but-myself culture, we need to be reminded that we need each other and that God needs us. We can serve Him with our relational skills by winning women, teaching women, helping them grow, and enlisting them in ministry and missions. A woman who hath friends is a woman of influence.

18

Be Blessed

*A*t a conference, I shared a room with Lynn, another workshop leader. She was single, in her early 30s, and a religious professional. She told me she lived alone and that she traveled extensively doing workshops and seminars.

We clicked immediately because we were both interested in personal prayer and Bible study. What fun we had discussing details and observations with someone who shared our enthusiasm! Our conversations were the epitome of what I've described in this book.

As we talked, I got to know Lynn. She was very intense about pleasing God, and I was touched by her devotion. I didn't see how any person could be more earnest and dedicated.

After one of the main conference sessions where the speaker spoke on total dependence on Christ, Lynn and I returned to our room. She asked, "May I talk with you about something very personal?"

"Well, sure, Lynn."

She began to cry as she told me that she had really tried to depend totally on Jesus, but there were times when she got extremely lonely. She said, "What is wrong with me that I cannot let Jesus be everything to me?"

I answered, "Oh, Lynn, nothing is wrong with you. God never intended for any of us to live the Christian life alone. Even Jesus needed others." She looked skeptical, so I talked about Jesus's relationships.

Jesus's need

"Jesus increased in wisdom and stature, and in favour with God and man*"* (Luke 2:52 KJV, author's emphasis). He was a social person, living with and interacting with family members and residents of Nazareth until He was 30. After He left home, He asked others to accompany Him. He needed assistants to preach and to exercise God's power (Mark 3:14c–15a), but He also chose them *"that they might be with him"* (Mark 3:14 NIV). Jesus needed companionship.

As His popularity exploded, crowds surrounded Him, but they came and went. They fluctuated in their attachment to Him. He needed companions who would be dependable and loyal; He called them His friends (John 15:15).

Needy people continuously approached Jesus, seeking something from Him. Some Galilean women befriended Him. They traveled with Him, supported Him and were present at the Cross (Luke 8:1–3; 23:49; Mark 15:40–41).

Other friends included Mary, Martha, and Lazarus; He knew them so well that He visited in their home. The Bible says that He loved them (John 11:5).

At crucial times, Jesus took time out for solitude, to commune with God and to be refreshed. The majority of the time during His ministry years, though, He was surrounded by steady, faithful companions. You can tell in His last conversations with them how very much He loved them (John 14, 15, and 16). They enriched His life and ministry, they assisted Him with His work, and together they had many insightful conversations.

Lynn's skeptical look never left her face, so I don't think I convinced her that it is all right to need others. Have I convinced you?

Not either or

In this book, I hope I have convinced you that it is not only all right to need others, but it is advantageous to do so. To be sure, our lives need times of solitude, the same kinds of solitary experiences Jesus had, but Jesus always returned to a life of companionship. It is not a matter of either or—a matter of God being everything or people being everything. It is God's plan that we have *both* in our lives with God always taking top priority, always occupying first place.

In other words, our people connections—whether it is family, co-workers, fellow church members, or friends—should never replace connecting with Jesus. They should never be a substitute for Him. Sometimes in reading about the friendships of women, the accolades can be so great that they begin to sound like the end-all and be-all of our existence, but they aren't. They form *one aspect* of our lives, an aspect that moving from one state to another raised my consciousness about. That's when I realized what an important part others play in determining the quality of life's journey. In looking back and in looking forward, I recognized the need women have to connect and to converse.

> I encourage solitude and recommend it ...but I also recommend time out with people. We need time to talk, to have unhurried, face-to-face conversations.

Following Jesus's example, I encourage solitude and recommend it in my speaking and writing,[1] but I also recommend time out with people. We need time to talk, to have unhurried, face-to-face conversations where we can experience the power of conversation.

The power of conversation

It has been said that one of life's greatest pleasures is the ability to speak. It enhances our lives and contributes to our sense of well-being! It can also bring us relief during times of stress, endurance during challenging times, and understanding as we negotiate the various stages of life. Conversation has the ability to change our lives and the lives of others. The power is evident when getting work done or when we want to expand our opportunities for experiencing God. Conversation also gives us an important tool for outreach. With words, we can win friends and influence women.

This is not to say that claiming the power of conversation is simple or easy. While women are blessed with a verbal specialty, that doesn't necessarily mean we have an instinctual ability to make connections. We may not know how, or we're stymied by fears. Others of us have lifestyles that don't appear to have room for unhurried conversations. If we want to experience the power of conversation, we have to find the time, become approachable, face our fears, take action, and be gracious. Making the effort is worth it because when a woman has other women she can talk with, she benefits in many ways.

The benefits of connecting and conversing

Her life is enriched. Enrichment is like adding cream and sugar to your coffee or adding Mandarin oranges and pecans to your chicken salad. The items are not necessary, but oh, what a difference in the taste! Unhurried, face-to-face conversations do the same for a woman's life. They aren't necessary to living; a woman will survive, but oh, what a difference conversations make in her enjoyment of life!

Her loneliness is reduced. I read in the newspaper of a poet who wrote to a friend of many years, "When you write my epitaph, you must say I was the loneliest person who ever lived." How sad! All of us experience loneliness of various kinds at different times in our lives. It is part of living, but no woman has to be lonely her whole life. She can make the effort to connect face-to-face and do something about loneliness.

Her stress is reduced. Our connections and conversations soothe our tumultuous inner world when we get a chance to release our thoughts and feelings, especially when we have a listener who responds with "I know how you feel."

Her spirit is lifted. Conversations help us remember who we really are, what we stand for and what we believe. Confidence in ourselves and in God can be restored and renewed when we talk with others.

She finds confidence and courage. Life presents difficulties from time to time so it can seem like we are just muddling through. As Paul said, *"Now we see through a glass, darkly"* (1 Corinthians 13:12 KJV). But getting from here to where we will see Jesus face-to-face, conversation with others can help us see where to walk and how to walk. Our vision becomes clearer and our step stronger.

Her influence is widened. Because she can minister through conversation, a woman need never feel like there's nothing she can do for God. The skills she gains in being friendly enable her to engage in influential conversations, whether they are with someone exactly like herself or someone completely different.

Her joy is increased. In writing about friendships in *Connecting: The Enduring Power of Female Friendship*, Sandy Sheehy said, "when women friends connect, we experience a spark, part exhilaration, part affirmation, that is intensely pleasant." That's the joy of connecting, and there's also joy in being women of influence. Nothing else matches the joy of seeing someone you are connecting with learn more about Jesus or become more like Him.

She grows. Our connections and conversations help shape who we are and who we are yet to be. The women we converse with care for us, confront us, and help us do things we never thought we could. As one survey respondent said, "Dear, dear friends are part of who I am."

Laura, another respondent, wrote, "Sisterhood is powerful. While society says to focus on children and men, women really need women. A female friend is not simply a last resort when husband is out of town and there's no soccer game. Her relationship fills a need and fosters growth like nothing else." I agree. And I hope after reading this book that you agree also. If you do, pick up a phone, call a girlfriend, and say, "Can you meet me for lunch?"

---

[1] I devote six chapters about Jesus's need for and use of solitude in *Reaching Heaven: Discovering the Cornerstones of Jesus' Prayer Life.* This need for time alone is one of the cornerstones of His prayer life.

Bibliography

Berkowitz, Gale. "UCLA Study on Friendship Among Women." http://www.rapereliefshelter.bc.ca/services/ucla_study_friendship.html

Berman, Dennis K. "Technology Has Us So Plugged Into Data, We Have Turned Off." *The Wall Street Journal*, November 10, 2003, page B1.

Brothers, Dr. Joyce. "Our Friends." *Parade*, February 16, 1997, pages 4–6.

Browder, Sue Ellin. "You Gotta Have Friends." *Woman's Day*, April 19, 1005, 46, 50, 52–53.

Burns, Stephen. "What's a Lonely Person to Do?" *Discipleship Journal*, November/December 2007, pages 42–48.

Courtney, Camerin J. "Unexpected Friends." *Today's Christian Woman*, November/December, 1996, pages 66–68.

Churchill, Theresa. "Decatur Woman Awarded for Efforts That Reach Across Races." *Herald & Review*, Decatur, Illinois, May 7, 2005, pages A1–A2.

Davis, Diana. *Fresh Ideas for Women's Ministry*. Nashville, Tennessee: Broadman and Holman, 2008.

Engelthaler, Lesa. "Putting Out the Welcome Mat: Lesa Engelthaler Interviews Randy Frazee." *Discipleship Journal*, November/December 2007, pages 50–55.

Goodman, Ellen, and Patricia O'Brien. *I Know Just What You Mean*. New York: Simon & Schuster, 2000.

Graham, Lorna. "Wanna Talk?" *Reader's Digest*, October 2003, pages 157–160.

Hales, Dianna. "The Female Brain." *Ladies' Home Journal*, May 1998, pages 128, 129, 173, 176, 184.

Jeffrey, Nancy Ann. "Whatever Happened to Friendship?" *The Wall Street Journal*, March 3, 2000, pages W1–W12.

Johnson, Jane Struck. "Doing Life Together." *Today's Christian Woman*, March/April 2001, pages 64–67.

Johnson, Jane Struck. "Building Deep Connections." *Today's Christian Woman*, March/April 2001, page 67.

Kuchment, Anna. "The More Social Sex." *Newsweek*, May 10, 2004, pages 88–89.

Laing, Kathleen and Elizabeth Butterfield. *Girlfriends' Getaway*. Colorado Springs, CO: WaterBrook Press, 2002.

Mains, David and Steve Bell, "Partners in Prayer," *Today's Christian Woman*, Nov.–Dec., 1991, pages 68–71.

Marshall, Melinda. "The Healing Power of Friendship." *Ladies' Home Journal*, February 2003, pages 69, 70, 72.

Poinsett, Brenda. *I'm Glad I'm a Woman*. Wheaton, Illinois: Tyndale House Publishers, 1988.

Poinsett, Brenda. *Why Do I Feel This Way?: What Every Woman Needs to Know About Depression*. Colorado Springs, Colorado: NavPress, 1996.

Robaina, Holly Vincente. "Isolation Nation." *Today's Christian Woman*, July/August 2007, pages 38–40.

Schmidt, Dan. "Paul & Friends." *Discipleship Journal*, Issue 106, July/August 1998, pages 33–36.

Sheehy, Sandy. *Connecting: The Enduring Power of Female Friendship*. New York: William Morrow, 2000.

Smalley, Erin and Carrie Oliver. *Grown-Up Girlfriends*. Carol Stream, Illinois: Tyndale House Publishers, 2007.

Smith, Cheryl M. *Kindling a Kindred Spirit: A Woman's Guide to Intimate Christian Friendship*. Camp Hill, Pennsylvania: Christian Publications, 1996.

Solomon, Andrew. *The Noonday Demon: An Atlas of Depression*. New York: Scribner, 2001.

Taylor, Shelley E. *The Tending Instinct: Women, Men, and the Biology of Our Relationships*. New York, New York: Times Books, Henry Holt and Company, LCC, 2002.

"You've Got a Friend." *St. Louis Post-Dispatch*, September 11, 2005, page EV2.

Webster, Douglas D. *Soulcraft: How God Shapes Us Through Relationships*. Downers Grove, Illinois: InterVarsity Press, 1999.

Widenhouse, Kathy. "The Power of a Positive Word," *Today's Christian Woman*, May/June 2002, pages 56–58.

Zaslow, Jeffrey. "Staying in Touch: One More Thing That Women Are Better at than Men." *The Wall Street Journal*, June 24, 2003, page D1.

If you've been blessed by this book, we would like to hear your story. The publisher and author welcome your comments and suggestions at: newhopereader@wmu.org.